THE ELLISON TREATMENT

written by
HARLAN ELLISON°

a Preservation Project production
for Harlan Ellison Books

edited by
Jason Davis

an
Edgeworks Abbey
offering

2019

THE ELLISON TREATMENT
is an Edgeworks Abbey® offering in association with
The Harlan Ellison Books Preservation Project.
Published by The Kilimanjaro Corporation.

To order definitive Ellison books, visit:
www.HarlanEllisonBooks.com

Assistant Editor: Cynthia Davis

ISBN: 978-1-946542-04-5

FIRST EDITION

Thanks to David Gerrold, Bo Nash & Michael Reed.

201904011350

CONTENTS

1   Harlan in Hollywood by Jason Davis

3   *Ripcord*: Four Premises

7   *Empire*: A Coat-Tail Ride Is the Smoothest Ride

13   *Airport*: An Ivory Mischief, a Silent Deceit

19   *Alfred Hitchcock Presents*:
Ormond Always Pays His Bills

21   *The Untouchables*: No More Saints

39   *The Great Adventure*:
Eight Bombs in Search of a Target

47   *Route 66*: One Life, Furnished in Early Poverty

67   *Route 66*: The Girl in the Spinning Glass Globe

75   *The Dick Powell Show*: All That Glitters

79   *Run for the Stars*

99   *The Alfred Hitchcock Hour*:
The Darkness Behind Their Eyes

109   *Honey West*: Mrs. Pigsfoot

117   *Amos Burke, Secret Agent*:
In the Valley of the Winds

129   *The Name of the Game*:
The Whimper of Whipped Dogs

133   *The Sixth Sense*: Salamander

137   *The Super*: The Star

139   *Land of the Lost*: The Guardians of the Pit

141   *Duck Tales*:
The Fowlness at the Center of the Earth!

Harlan in
Hollywood

In early 1962, Harlan Ellison arrived in Hollywood. After conning his way into the offices of General Artists Corporation and securing representation in the form of Stuart Robinson and Martin Shapiro, Ellison began to make the rounds, pitching story premises to various shows gearing up for the 1962–1963 television season. But before we get to what he pitched to whom, a couple points of order:

Ellison wrote in the 18 April 1969 installment of his column, *The Glass Teat*, "a script assignment for tv is divided into three parts: treatment, first draft, final draft. You can be 'cut off' after the treatment, meaning they pay you only for what you have already written, and the assignment is dead." THE ELLISON TREATMENT collects a selection of these cut-off storylines, scenarios that fell at the first hurdle. The attentive reader may note certain recurring motifs, ideas that didn't sell to show A later being pitched to show B (or indeed, show C); waste not, want not.

I've attempted to array the treatments herein in chronological order. Annoyingly, the author didn't start dating his work until he landed a steady gig at *Burke's Law* in April 1963, so the first year's worth of screenwriting has been sequenced to the best of the editor's ability, using clues like the aforementioned recurring plots and typographical arcana that only a disturbed person would notice.

Ripcord was Ellison's first stop on the pitch parade. A syndicated series created by Harry Redmond, Jr. and Jim Hall and produced by Ziv-United Artists, the show starred Larry Pennell and Ken Curtis as skydiving instructors Ted McKeever and Jim Buckley. Ellison came armed with four potential premises for the series, one of which— "Where Do the Elephants Go to Die?"—became his first teleplay to air. [The final result was published in BRAIN MOVIES, Volume 5.] The beginner's luck, alas, did not hold.

TO BE CONTINUED...

Ripcord

four premises

(1962)

FALL DOWN, PLAY DEAD

They went through Korea together, and in their own way they're a pair of trained killers. Rog had saved Yorkey's life and though they've been kicking around since the "police action," mostly getting into trouble, cracking up cars and generally raising hell, Rog and Yorkey are ace-high buddies, and as Yorkey put it, "You 'n' me, buddy. We're goin' through this scene back-to-back, what I got...you can have; ain't *nothin'* I wouldn't do for the guy who saved my life." So when Rog decides he wants to be a skydiver, and takes lessons with Ted and Jim, Yorkey calls him a nut, but wishes him well. Then Rog thinks he's past teaching, ignores the French Frog and does a bullet-dive, and spreads himself across three acres of alfalfa. Yorkey decides to get the guy that killed his buddy. He takes up with Ted where Rog left off, planning for McKeever a Siamese twin of what happened to Rog. Inevitably, on the assassination flight, Yorkey pulls a pistol on Ted and tells him he's going down the hard way, sans chute. He explains why. Ted denies responsibility for Rog's death, explains that Rog panicked and was too scared to pull the ripcord. Yorkey nearly tears Ted's head off with the muzzle of the gun: Not *my* buddy, McKeever. Anybody else, yeah, sure,

3

I can believe it...but not Rog. We went through hell together and there wasn't anybody that could scare him, or any*thing*. You just don't want to admit you sent him off ill-trained. We had guys like you in Korea." He starts to edge Ted toward the port, minus chute. Ted jumps him and they go out together, only Yorkey wearing silk. They fall together, and Yorkey freezes, cannot pull the ripcord...they fall...Ted tries to cling to the assassin and pull the cord himself...they fall...he can't seem to reach it...they fall...Yorkey unfreezes, begins to thrash as...they fall... Ted manages to pull the cord...they land hard, but Yorkey and Ted are alive. The ex-hero from Korea sits huddled on the ground, shivering, realizing he was incapable of action, in effect a coward. Ted helps him up, talks to him tightly and makes him realize that in every one of us who is walking, there is a terrified little man who is crawling, and most of us never have to face that moment when we learn whether we're walking erect or crawling. Yorkey abruptly knows what it means to be afraid. The tiger has learned to fear. And he knows that the largest part of the bravado he and Rog had displayed was simple bullying and sham. McKeever had told the truth...Rog *had* been scared...and so, in fact, had he...and it's good to know when to be afraid.

OH! YOU GOLDEN BIRD!

A gorgeous showgirl, intent on making a name for herself through fair means or foul, splashes publicity for her new act as "The Golden Bird Girl"in every local newspaper, announcing she will delay-drop wearing a pair of golden gull-wings, à la Icarus. She cons Ted and Jim into going along with her scheme, not bothering to tell them that the aerodynamic design for the Golden Bird Wings was stolen from an engineer she had duped.

WHERE DO THE ELEPHANTS GO TO DIE?

When you're dying of cancer, and your last days are laid out like soup spoons, and you have the guts to want to die like a man, not like a machine running down, how do you plan your own end? Do you submerge yourself in drink and wild women and a fast life? Do you crawl off into a seedy rooming-house and brood about the Reaper coming for you? Or do you finally decide to go out in a splash, from a skydiving plane? And if you do, what right do your friends McKeever and Buckley have trying to stop you? After all, it's *your* life, even if you are a Nobel Prize-winning novelist with a great gift for the world. So get out of the way...

THE FALL OF THE FUNNY MAN

McKeever and Buckley are engaged to appear on a late-night variety show (in the Paar manner) and once on-camera are treated to a degrading exchange of wisecracks by the comedian who emcees the show. He calls skydivers out of their minds and remarks, "These skydiving nuts go through three stages—young weirdies, middle-aged sickies, and old kooks—if they live that long!" Ted blows up, on the air, and challenges the funnyman to take a few jumps, if he thinks it's all for the birds. The comedian accepts, and Ted finds he has more trouble than he bargained for. (This show could explore the question of whether or not a public figure has the right to express such a colored opinion through mass media.)

Empire, created by Kathleen Hite, was an hour-long modern-day Western centered on the exploits of Jim Redigo (Richard Egan), the manager of a 500,000-acre New Mexico ranch. Produced by Screen Gems, it was broadcast on NBC from 25 September 1962 to 14 May 1963. [NOTE: The lead character's name was either in flux or misheard by Ellison when he composed his treatment, in which it appears as RETIGO.]

Though Ellison's eight-page treatment for "A Coat-Tail Ride Is the Smoothest Ride" is undated, the mention of Lucia Garrett (Anne Seymour), the ranch owner for whom Redigo worked, indicates that the storyline was written early in the first season, before the character was killed off. As with much of Sixties television, the plot focused on the guest characters, so when this storyline failed to secure a teleplay commitment from *Empire*, Ellison struck out the title and planned to sell the premise—with appropriate character and venue adjustments—to *Airport*...

A Coat-Tail Ride Is
the Smoothest Ride
Empire (1962)

FADE IN as ex-senator Joe Kilkenny stalks away from the camera, fists flailing the air, back taut with fury, voice raised in anger. "The *devil* you say, boy! You'll run, by God! You'll run, and you'll win! Your brothers made it and *you* can make it...Kilkenny is a big name in this state...maybe the biggest...yes, by God, it *is* the biggest! Oh, you'll run, all right; or you'll find out trouble comes bigger than you can handle! You're not too old to whup, you know!"

The object of his tirade, Lyle "Buddy" Kilkenny, youngest of the three heirs to the Kilkenny political duchy, sits silently, listening, seething. He is a placid-faced but personable man, formed in the very mold of contemporary clean-cut young American dynamism...a prime example of what the in-fighters of the political arena call "mass-marketable": Ivy-cut hair, conservative dress, alert expression and bearing, with just enough ruggedness in the jaw and cheek lines to express honesty, forthrightness, and courage—but not enough to suggest animosity or stubbornness. Everybody's clever younger brother; everybody's confidante. In short, Buddy Kilkenny is prime candidate timber, a shoo-in for tv and public office.

He watches his father, half-fearful, half-defiant, but with a tinge of jelly in his expression that gives him away. He is a man—well, not *quite* a man, but close enough to fool the not-too-perceptive—under strain, at a moment of crisis. A moment in which the quicksand upon which his temperament has been formed may give way.

"Now look, Dad..." he murmurs.

"Don't *now look Dad* me, Buddy. This seat in the House is up for grabs, and by all that's holy you'll go out for it, and you'll win!" The older man stalks to the fireplace in the huge, paneled drawing-room, and begins packing a pipe with spastic, violent movements. Suddenly he turns: "You'll win, or—"

"Or *what*?" Buddy Kilkenny pushes out of his chair with unrestrained anger. "Or *what*, Dad? Will you fire me? Will you revoke my birth certificate? Will you take away my name?"

The older man's expression alters subtly. He wants to express affection, confidence, communicate in some way that there is more at stake here than just a seat in the House of Representatives. But he is a prisoner of his skin, a man unable to express affection in normal terms. "Sometimes I can't understand you," he ventures, lamely.

"What's to understand?" Buddy spreads his hands. "I'm not my brother Steve, the right honorable Governor of this state, and I'm not my brother Dave, Senior Senator from this glorious state. I'm me, and I'm a bum...so what the devil do you want from me?"

The fight is interrupted by Dana Kilkenny, Buddy's wife, a slim, blonde woman with the figure of a high fashion model, the aloof chilled bearing of a Countess, and a smoldering animal brightness that peers out from behind the chipped-ice eyes. "Dad," she says to her father-in-law, "Buddy's been very upset about this. Why not give him some time to think about it?"

"Time?" explodes the senior Kilkenny. "*Time?*" he pounds the mantelpiece with a fist that still retains its power, despite the years of use pummeling conference tables. "He's had nothing *but* time. We have to get the wheels in motion...time is running out...I want that seat!"

"Yeah, *you* do, but *I* don't!" Buddy Kilkenny snaps a finger at his father. "I'm afraid I'll fall off the sanctified, holy coat-tails of my elder brothers, and I just flat-out don't want it! Now *leave me alone!*"

He stalks toward the oak double-doors. "Where are you going?" his father demands. Buddy Kilkenny pauses, hand on doorknob.

"I'm going up to see Jim Retigo. I need some fresh air. The smell of power politics is making me sick."

The man and woman watch him as he whips the door open, and as it violently slams closed, flash

MAIN TITLE: EMPIRE

AND CREDITS

Buddy goes to hide-out temporarily at the ranch run by Retigo. There he expresses his fears, conflicting and many-dimensioned, to Retigo and Lucia, that he wants to do research on the Navajo Indians, that he does not want to run for office and become a public figure, that he hates the smear campaign he knows will follow from the opposition when they learn that the youngest Kilkenny is trying to hop on the gravy-train. Retigo expresses concern, but inability to solve his problems, yet extends to Buddy the run of the ranch, for as long as he wishes to remain a guest.

The days pass with Buddy throwing himself into a round of chores that make him think even more deeply about his problem. His love is anthropology, he wants to go out in the field and work with the people, not remain cloistered in a dreary political monastery. But the pressures are invading, even at the ranch.

First the telegrams.

Then the phone calls.

Then Joe Kilkenny comes to visit, and stays to harass his son. He tries to get Retigo to convince the boy, knowing their days together in college, and their strong mutual admiration, make Retigo the deciding voice as Buddy swings back and forth in a breeze of indecision.

Retigo tells Joe Kilkenny he is not entirely sure Buddy should *be* placed in a position of responsibility; he intimates that it is not only because of Buddy's desires, but because he feels Buddy has not matured, that he has been shadowed by his brothers for so long, bludgeoned by his father's indomitable will for so long, that he has not been fully formed as a man.

Then comes the magazine reporter, planning an article titled "Little Brother Buddy at the Post." Upon hearing the insipid slant of the piece,

Buddy becomes infuriated and beats the reporter soundly, sending him away swearing to write a piece that will make the youngest Kilkenny look like the infant he is.

Buddy Kilkenny takes a jeep and flees into the New Mexico hills, seeking an escape that does not exist outside himself. Retigo and Lucia's daughter go in search of him, find him wandering the hills crying, seeking some innocence of childhood or nature that he has lost. They take him back to the ranch, only to find Dana waiting.

In a scene of uncontrolled fury, Dana reveals to Joe Kilkenny and Retigo that if Buddy does not run, she is leaving him. Her true nature— barely concealed till now—shows itself. She is a woman incapable of true love, a woman whose *noblesse oblige* has been so warped that all the trappings of position and reputation are important, while the human beings involved are dust. She tells them her life is planned, on a timetable, and she's wasted enough years with Buddy. If he doesn't pay off, she will have to move on to greener pastures.

Kilkenny tries to argue with her, telling her it will ruin Buddy's chances for ever making office if he is divorced. Neither of them really understand Retigo's anger as he tells them they are thinking of Buddy as six pounds of horsemeat and not as a person. They are trying to use him and must ruin him if they continue.

Buddy overhears it all, and explodes once more, but this time in a paroxysm of revelation in which he expresses his insecurity and fear, saying, "There's safety in being mediocre; there's peace and security in not being loved. I don't have to compete. I don't have to fight other people's battles."

The implication, brought out by Dana, is that Buddy is not man enough to have any battles of his own.

They go their separate ways, and later that night Dana comes to Jim Retigo's rooms, in an attempt not only to seduce him, but to get him to convince Buddy he should run. Retigo accepts her advances, joins her passion, right up to the moment that she becomes excited, then tosses her down roughly, expressing his contempt for her. "As far as I can figure, you're only good for a handful of things, Dana, and from looking at you, I don't suppose you even do any of *them* very well.

"It's frightening to see a woman's body with no woman in it," he concludes, stalking out into the night.

The next day, Lucia suggests the group go out into the hills hunting javelina, the dangerous killer-pigs that infest the caves. She expresses her feelings that a hunt may take the edge off everyone, and Retigo realizes that she has been—at least in part—a witness to the scene with Dana the night before.

They go into the hills, and in a cave high in the back country they discover a pack of javelina, hidden at the rear of the cave. Retigo warns them that when the pigs surge out, their long teeth can rip a man's legs off. He warns everyone to stand clear, and fires a shot into the rear of the cave.

The javelina charge, and in the scuffle, Buddy panics, firing wildly, then breaking and running, directly in front of the charging beasts. Retigo manages to save him, but Dana begins to laugh, and charges her husband with being a coward and a weakling, too laughable ever to make a good servant of the people.

Buddy lashes out at her, knocking her to the ground, cursing and pledging he'll run for office, and win, and show the entire family, as well as the world, that he's a man.

Then Retigo says, "But you're *not* a man, Buddy. You're not Lyle, you're Buddy, a kid...it's not so much your fault as other people's, but when the times came to say *I'm ready to grow up*, you didn't have the nerve. Now it's too late."

Buddy vows he'll run, infuriated at Retigo's opposition. But Joe Kilkenny steps in, sadness etched in his face, all his years and hopes and struggles suddenly come to this. "No, Buddy, you won't run. Not without my help, and I'm withdrawing it. I don't know whether to be sorry or ashamed. For too long now I've seen somebody else whenever I looked at you. But now I see you, and I did a lousy job of making a man of you."

He walks away.

"Go study your Indians, Buddy," Dana tells him. And she, too, leaves him, lost, alone, without a future.

And then Buddy Kilkenny, standing alone in the hills, swears he will do it. Without the help of the machine, without the power and prestige of the Kilkenny name. Retigo hears him in the approaching dusk, vowing to the sky that he'll do it, and he smiles.

Without crutches, a man who imagines himself a cripple, must either walk or fall. There is room to hope Buddy Kilkenny will walk. Haltingly, at first, perhaps, but at least on two feet, not all four, like a baby.

Airport has proven something of a mystery. Aside from Ellison's repurposed plot from *Empire* and an aborted storyline titled "An Ivory Mischief, a Silent Deceit," your editor hasn't found so much as a scintilla of evidence this series ever existed. Given that studios and networks sometimes commission additional stories or scripts before committing to a new series, it's reasonable to conjecture that this unfinished treatment was set aside when the powers that be opted not to move forward with the series. [That was certainly the case with *My Name Is Adam*—AKA *Postmark: Jim Adam*, AKA *Postmark: Jim Fletcher*—a series for which Ellison wrote two-and-a-half treatments, though only the pilot episode was produced and broadcast.]

The story, a meditation on what Hollywood does to beautiful women who come seeking their fortune, would become a recurring theme in Ellison's work over the next several years, culminating with "The Resurgence of Miss Ankle-Strap Wedgie."

An Ivory Mischief,
a Silent Deceit

Airport (1962)

Aristotle called beauty "the gift of God,"
Socrates called it "a short-lived tyranny,"
Theophrastus, "a silent deceit" and
Theocritus "an ivory mischief."

Grumman waits at Gate 13, thinking: *Marlene Blaine will be coming through here any moment now; the star, going home after her conquest of Glitter City. I was here a year ago, too, at her arrival. What was it like then...when she was fresh and new...*

Bedlam! A jamming, shoving, hysterical crowd that threatens to break through the cyclone fences at Gate 13. Reporters, a dozen of them, plunged to the forefront of the mob, press flashes held high to avoid getting them smashed, eyes trained on the stretch of tarmac upon which the incoming flight will land. Airport guards arm-locked to keep the horde back. And Grumman, intense and ready, on the other side of the fence only because he is the PR voice of International Airport, but electric with anticipation, like his comrades of the Fourth Estate.

What dignitary or celebrity is due to arrive? What controversial figure or resident of the underworld? What decider of men's fate will soon come jetting in?

Then the silver streak of the Boeing arcs across the field, the crowd goes a little madder, the approach, the wheels skin rubber, the huge jetliner skitters to a halt and rolls into its berth...and the mob breaks loose. No holding them, no restraining them as they burst through the fence-gate and pour out across the field. Grumman, too, impelled to keep his beat on this important story, races along with them, managing to get into the very phalanx of the mob.

And then, almost as though on cue, the crowd pours into the area around the aluminum staircase and stops, breathless, waiting, as the ground crew prepares to unseal the plane.

Finally the port swings open, the stewardess and the co-pilot stand aside, and the *Arrivals* begin to step out! The crowd goes wild... flashbulbs pop...whistles rise on the wind...applause...

One, two, three, ten, fifteen, twenty, twenty-one...

Twenty-one gorgeous girls, the only commodity that could drag out so many anxious men, so many hot-rock reporters who know what sells newspapers. Twenty-one extraordinarily beautiful girls, contestants in the 1961 Miss L. A. International Airport competition. Twenty-one dolls from all over the world, gathered here to get a chance at the ephemeral ghost of success, fame, prestige, and romance. The girl who wins gets a one-year contract with a major film company, she gets feted and publicized, wined and dined, adored and coo'ed over. For a brief candle-moment in time she is The Queen.

Gopher presses up next to Grumman. "Wow!" is all he can muster. That much beauty, all in one place, is too staggering for coherent comment. "Gopher," Grumman says, "when the hullabaloo dies down, I want *that* one, *that* one, and *that* one," and he points at the three most arresting girls in the group.

"I'm going to take a calculated risk, Gopher. Those three look the best to me, and I'd bet *one* of them will win this sweepstake. But just to make sure, I'm going to do columns on all three of them, follow them around L. A., see who they meet, what they do, what becomes of them, and you know, I think we're going to get a story out of this that no one else has really done. I think we're going to find out what stardust can do to a beautiful girl in Hollywood."

ACT ONE:

The three girls are totally unlike one another.

Harriet Pershing, a honey-blonde with wide, innocent gray eyes; a cool and distant-looking girl, long-legged and the very apotheosis of high fashion. The iceberg girl, with a regal beauty that makes men automatically put her on a pedestal. The sort of woman for whom men battle Philistine hordes, with nothing but the jawbone of an ass as weapon.

Kearney Kohler, who casts the most perfect contemporary image of them all. She is truly the girl in the soap ad, the all-time fun chick seen in the soda pop commercial. She loves to do the Twist, loves to ride faster than the fastest car can ride, is the one who says, "I simply haven't a *thing* to wear," the one who loves quickly, frenziedly, over and over again. Gamin-like, auburn-haired, insouciant, and compelling, she has the twinkle, the bounce, the verve that makes men turn and stare at her on the street—without knowing they are smiling happily. She is the incarnation of fun & games in woman. Bright-eyed and bushy-tailed she sails through life finding opals, rubies, and amethysts in the dustiest coal piles.

and...

Marlene Blaine, the most exquisite girl you've ever seen.

The girl who knows what she wants.

The girl who will get it.

With a barely discernable touch of hardness about her, she *will* have the Good Life, even if it entails shaving the ethics and morality a little thin, even if it involves going the body route, even if it demands cunning and cleverness and subterfuge. The man-eater, the barracuda, the girl with the solid steel teeth, with the eye on the horizon and the hand on the pulse of fame and fortune. Capable of soft, feminine affection or anthracite-hard commando action, this girl instinctively knows you're not judged on how you got there, only where you are. It's not the years, it's the miles, and this girl wants to ride, not walk.

Grumman watched these three—after his initial interviews with them—watches them as they go through their paces at the contest. And he is not surprised when Marlene wins. She was *bound* to win, it had to be.

But he continues his series on all three, for to Grumman it is equally as important to know what happens to the losers as to the winner. Only forty per cent of the girls who come to L. A. each year To Hit It Big ever return home. What becomes of the other sixty per cent...?

This is what happens:

Marlene's screen test comes through and though her talent is not that dazzling, her appearance is, and she begins to fall in with the Hollywood fast set—producers with casting couches and big plans that entail much talk and little money; actors who spend their time in coffee houses talking about their art; weirdos who live on the seamy underside of Los Angeles life; the impressionable and the debauched. She uses them as they use her. Grumman writes a column on her after spending several days in her company, seeing who she knows and what she does.

Then he leaves her and moves on to Kearney, who has taken a job as a car-hop in a drive-in. She is beginning to feel the press of dissatisfaction and unhappiness; her dreams have evaporated. The big future has dwindled to petty problems of rent and clothes and transportation and the reality that three meals a day must be consumed to stay alive. Kearney is becoming bitter, for she cannot return to Sioux City and let the friends and relatives who saw her off know she has failed. So she persists in her dreary life, just another of the beautiful girls snared by Hollywood.

Harriet, on the other hand, has denied the phony glamor, has decided *any* town is a good town if you know who you are, if you decide what you want out of life. She has taken a job as a receptionist for a publicity firm, and is modeling in her spare time. She is meeting people and establishing a routine, an existence for herself.

Grumman's three articles appear on three subsequent days, and each girl's life is drastically changed by the notice the pieces attract.

ACT TWO:

Marlene, whose career had been going nowhere, though she was being seen around town, suddenly takes a firm step forward. Interest is generated in her because of the newspaper column, and she is cast in a secondary, but juicy, role in a major production. She calls Grumman, invites him down to the set to do another piece on her. He goes, finds she has become impressed with her own publicity, that she believes the image the studio has built for her, and decides not to do a follow-up on her. Angry about his "preaching" and concluding he is giving her the sour grapes treatment just because she has hit it, Marlene orders him off the set.

Grumman seeks out Kearney, who has taken up with the hangers-on at P. J.'s and the Raincheck. She tells him she

EDITOR'S NOTE: This treatment was apparently abandoned before Ellison completed it. The extant copy ends, abruptly.

Having already placed "Memo(s) from Purgatory"—based on his 1961 memoir MEMOS FROM PURAGTORY—with *Alfred Hitchcock Presents*, Ellison followed up with a pitch based on his 1957 crime story, "Ormond Always Pays His Bills." While "Memo" eventually made it to the screen as an installment of the expanded and retitled *Alfred Hitchcock Hour* on 21 December 1964, "Ormond" remained undeveloped until 1984, when Ellison wrote the teleplay "Moonlighting" for a short-lived thriller anthology called *Scene of the Crime*. The Orson Welles-hosted series lasted for five episodes on NBC; Ellison's script was never produced, though it was published in SCREAMPLAYS (1997), edited by Richard Chizmar and Martin H. Greenberg.

The Untouchables, Desilu's hour-long fictionalization of Prohibition Agent Eliot Ness's exploits in 1930s Chicago, starred Robert Stack as Ness, and was entering it's last season on ABC when Ellison pitched "No More Saints." When Ellison's treatment failed to find favor, he filed away the plot mechanics based on the assassination of Mayor Anton Cermak, and resurrected them 35 years later for "Objects in Motion," a *Babylon 5* episode co-plotted and scripted by J. Michael Straczynski.

"Eight Bombs in Search of a Target" was based on Operation Pastorius, a 1942 German plan to infiltrate the USA. Ellison dramatized the story for *The Great Adventure*, a CBS anthology hosted by Van Heflin, which presented historical scenarios in a one-hour timeslot. As with the preceding plots, it failed. (At the time of his 2014 stroke, this treatment had been exhumed from Ellison's files and was on his desk; make of that what you will.)

The Screen Gems pseudo-anthology *Route 66*, created by Herbert B. Leonard and Stirling Silliphant, was Ellison's next destination. The series, which followed Tod Stiles (Martin Milner) and Buz Murdock (George Maharis) as they made their way across the USA, becoming involved in the lives of people they meet, was nearing the end of its road.

"The Hungriest Girl on the Scene"—later retitled "One Life, Furnished in Early Poverty," though unrelated to the short story of the same name—drew much of its background from Ellison's recent stint as an editor at *Rogue* magazine (1959–60), a theme that would continue in subsequent pitches. It's possible Ellison's storyline went off the road when Maharis left the series mid-season. Ellison's second scenario, "The Girl in the Spinning Glass Globe," was a solo adventure focusing on Tod Stiles, but it didn't find traction.

Ormond Always Pays His Bills

Alfred Hitchcock Presents (1962)

Hervey Ormond, largest building contractor in the county, has come to an inescapable conclusion. He must kill his secretary, Francine. She is the only one who knows how he bought one of the planning commissioners on the highway project for which Ormond won the construction bid. She is also the only one who knows where the proof lies that Ormond used inferior materials in the laying of the highway. Cement that was half sand, improper foundations, and cheapjack tarmac, callous disregard for the safety of the motorists who would be using the road...all of these have led to the shocking disintegration of the highway within three years of its construction. Compound criminal negligence, bribing a state official, prior knowledge of sealed bids, and collusion with intent to defraud and the fear of investigation Ormond suffers becomes greater than the horror of murder.

Yet why would Francine turn in her employer? Perhaps because she is Hervey Ormond's ex-paramour, a girl with whom he trifled for years, promising marriage, only to wed the daughter of the town's wealthiest man, to get ahead in a business that was failing through mismanagement and ineptitude.

Francine's love for Ormond has turned to vindictiveness, and in seeking revenge, she has anonymously approached the State's Attorney's

Office. Francine—in a moment of alcoholic self-pity—decides to give Ormond another chance. A chance to divorce his wife, make good his promises to her, and save himself from exposure and imprisonment. She calls Ormond, tells him to meet her at the office, and tells him if he wants to stay in circulation, he'd better agree.

Ormond comes to the office, and in a scene of vitriol and fury, Francine ridicules his mismanagement of the firm, his predilection for candy bars that have aided Ormond's race to near-obesity, and concludes by threatening him with scandal and prison if he doesn't meet her demands. Enraged, Ormond attacks her. Francine fights back and manages to trip Ormond. She laughs at him: "Can't even beat up a woman!"

Ormond grabs up an ornate brass lamp from his desk, a lamp whose heavy base is shaped like a bulldozer, a personalized gift that bears his name…and bludgeons her to death.

When he comes back to his senses, Hervey Ormond realizes he has lived all his days to come to this moment. He is a pudgy, frightened murderer, threatened from all sides.

Panic tears at him, then passes, and he begins to function. He devises a plan to be rid of Francine's body and the threat to his position. Gull Lake, at the other end of the county, is hundreds of feet deep. Francine could disappear into its muddy, dark waters and never be heard from again. He could tell the curious few who might ask for her (and she had never really made that many friends in town, after all), that she had gone to live with relatives in another state.

"But this time I'll make certain I do things right," Ormond vows. Not only will he dump her in Gull Lake, but he will sink her to the ankles in cement, tie the cord of the lamp to her, and sink her, with the murder weapon, forever from sight.

Ormond takes her body to his construction yard, stands her in a vat of ready-mix cement, and then when she is hardened in it, dumps her into the trunk of his car, takes her to the Lake, and throws her, with the lamp, into the deep.

He goes home and settles back with a handsomely guilty conscience that does not prevent him from beginning a new deal for a public building.

One week later, the state police come to arrest Hervey Ormond, for the murder of Francine.

He was clever, but unfortunately Francine had floated to the top. Ormond should never have used his own defective cement.

No More Saints

The Untouchables (ca. 1962–63)

TEASER

May 29th, 1930, Chicago, exactly seven months after Black Tuesday 1929, when the stock market pulled the trapdoor on itself and hung gasping while twenty-five million Americans lost fifty billion dollars.

The Chicago Yacht Basin, dim and twinkling against the waters of Lake Michigan, and on one sumptuous vessel lights blazing, crowd noise carrying across the evening, the sound of excellent Chi-style jazz rising over it all. Apparently the market crash has not ruined fun for everyone; a party.

Seated at a table by the side of a dance floor, Prosecuting Attorney Justin Carlyle sips bootleg champagne and taps his carefully-manicured fingers to the beat of the music, provided by Len & Brian Breslin, whose combo has been hired for this outing of the "400." At his side a post-deb both sleek and refined assures us that Justin Carlyle's taste in women is as discerning and discreet as his taste in music. Carlyle is a tall, dapper man, elegant in a polished way, with a hint of reserved deviltry that contrasts with his appearance.

As we move about the lounge of the palatial yacht, having established Carlyle, our narration tells us that after six years of trying to fruitlessly nail Enoch L. "Nucky" Johnson, biggest of the top hoods, on a bootlegging charge, Eliot Ness had stumbled across sufficient evidence to have him indicted for first degree murder, and that this same Justin Carlyle who sits among high society wastrels, is the man who will try the case. Winchell tells us that after six months of postponements and continuances, assaults by batteries of Machiavellian lawyers, unbelievable pressures both politically and personally—with "Nucky" Johnson held without bail all the while—now, 24 hours before the start of the trial, Justin Carlyle has been set by the friends of "Nucky" Johnson for a hit.

As these words are spoken we see a close-up of a champagne bucket, with something metallic being thrust down into the ice, being covered with more ice, then a jeroboam of champagne being twirled down into the ice, covering whatever secret thing lies hidden beneath. The ice bucket is lifted and we go with it, extreme close-up, to Justin Carlyle's table.

As our attention is attracted to the ice bucket being maneuvered in close to Carlyle, in the extreme foreground, the main action is Carlyle yelling across the small dance floor to the Breslin brothers.

"Play 'No More Saints'!" he enjoins them.

Brian Breslin is tall, and though as dark as his cornetist brother Len, there is a twinkle to him. Brian laughs through life. It's a gig, a big joke, intended to be lived without tears or frowns, but always with the sound of good music coming up from deep inside. He seems somehow the best of all possible choices when selecting a C-melody sax man. Len is more intense, a shorter, wiry man for whom music and his brother Brian are a way of life, a dedication. As softly amenable as Brian seems to be, that is how wire-spring taut Len is.

Yet there is love between them. In the way they look at each other as they play, in their total involvement with each other's music and movements, it is obvious that together they form a gestalt that neither alone could match.

As the applause from their ride-out finish on "Royal Garden Blues" dwindles, and they hear Justin Carlyle's shouted request, Len steps forward and announces they will play a song written by his brother Brian, a new number called "No More Saints"—and it's being dedicated to Mr. Justin Carlyle.

They begin to play, and as the haunting, sensual beat of the song winds in among the tinkle of shot glasses and the twitter of flapper giggles, the crowd falls silent.

For Len and Brian are talking to one another with this song. The cornet asks its imperative questions, and the mellow sax replies, picking up the melody and carrying it along gently. It is an easily-remembered, a quickly-recognized tune, but filled with sensitivity and deep emotionalism. It is a private statement of affection and need between these two men.

The crowd listens silently as "No More Saints" leads Len and Brian through their asking-answering melodic duologue, while the camera holds on them past Carlyle, the ominous ice bucket still huge in the foreground. And as the song ends, the crowd sits for a long moment before the applause breaks loose.

Carlyle rises, takes two steps toward the bandstand, enthusiastically applauding the brothers, and it is this sudden movement on his part that saves his life, for at that point the ice bucket with its bomb inside explodes, hurling Carlyle to the floor, sending the table crashing over on top of him.

As the concussion and report die away, as the rubble and smoke settle, Justin Carlyle pulls himself out from beneath the table, shrugs off roughly the hands that try to help him, and stares with open fury at the scene around him. The camera holds tightly on his face, his expression of determination, then goes with his POV as we see his girl friend, slumped against the wall, crying, hands over her face, as though she has been blinded by the explosion. And we know Justin Carlyle will not let this pass...

Carlyle reaches into his pocket for something as one of the dazed playboys in tuxedo smeared with dust and dirt stumbles by. He grabs the man, thrusts a nickel into his hand, and snaps, "Call the Federal Building; tell Eliot Ness I want to see him," he pauses, "at my office."

Fade out as Carlyle propels the playboy on his way and camera moves in for another angle of the prosecutor's intense, hard-muscled face.

ACT ONE

Fade in the silent Federal Building, a dim corridor as footsteps echo through the shadows. Eliot Ness strides down the hall, pauses a moment to pass a word with a cleaning woman scrubbing the floor, then moves on toward the only office that shows light through its glass pane.

He enters the office. Carlyle is poring over reams of pre-trial briefs. He does not wait for even a hello from Ness, but launches immediately into a series of question:

"Eliot, this witness who refuses to cooperate, what's his name—" he consults brief, "—Wallace Pranger..."

Ness is amazed. "Eleven o'clock at night, you've just had someone try to spread you out with a bomb, the trial opens day after tomorrow, and you're asking me about a man we've been trying to get to open up for six months...Jus, what are you trying to prove? You ought to be hidden away somewhere, letting the locals find who planted that bomb."

Carlyle waves away Ness's objections. "Eliot, don't lecture me, it's been a rough night, and I had a good party broken up by one of 'Nucky's' playmates. Now what about this Pranger, any developments?"

Ness resigns himself, "You want 'Nucky' as badly as I do, don't you, Jus?"

Carlyle nods tightly, remembering. "Worse, Eliot. Much worse. You got the case against him, but I've been fighting to see it into court for six months, through every possible maneuver and sandbagging technique 'Nucky's' operation could devise. And I want him strapped in that chair, Eliot; I want him off the streets for good."

They talk further, and Ness reminds Carlyle that he has been forbidden to work on the case any further by the federal government, that they contend Johnson's indictment is on a civil offense, though the information in the murder trial was gathered by Ness while in pursuit of evidence of Johnson's bootlegging activities.

Ness says he wants to put Carlyle under a special guard, that he wants the Untouchables to stay with him till the trial is over. Carlyle argues violently, saying he doesn't need any more protection, that the local police he has been assigned are doing the job. Eliot mentions the bomb, and Carlyle cannot argue. Eliot forces the D. A. to a compromise: if Carlyle will accept and abide by an Untouchable protection, he will call Washington, speak to the Commissioner of Prohibition, and try to get permission to continue with the case. Carlyle agrees, saying, "Do you think you can get Pranger to talk? He's maintained he knows nothing for six months." Ness assures Carlyle that Pranger actually saw the commission of the murder by "Nucky" Johnson, but has been threatened into silence, particularly at this late date. Carlyle becomes intense, says that what happened tonight at the boat makes him want Johnson even more than he'd thought he could.

Ness calls Washington, argues with his superiors, finally gets permission for himself and his Untouchables to continue in the case, to testify at the trial, and to guard Carlyle, on the grounds that he is of immeasurable value to the department.

When he hangs up, Carlyle grins at him, "Why don't we knock off for an hour or so and have a drink...after all, I don't want this perfectly good tuxedo to go to waste." Ness does not think the suggestion humorous. "You've got to stay out of the public scene for a few days, at least till the trial is over, Jus...all this night-clubbing makes you an open target."

Carlyle gets snappish: "Don't confuse my business life with my private life, Eliot. They run on two separate tracks." Ness does not answer. Carlyle tries to jolly him, "Come on, I'll buy." Ness answers tightly, "Let others close the speaks tonight, Jus. I'm staying here till Youngfellow and Rossi take over, then I've got my own work to do. Leave the speaks to those who belong in them..."

On which words we sharp cut to the bandstand of a smoky speakeasy, where Len and Brian Breslin are once more playing "No More Saints." As they tail off, they do not wait for the applause, but launch into a few bars of "Good Night Ladies" and leave the stand, allowing the other three members of the combo to finish the sign-off *a capella*.

The brothers pause in the wings for a moment, and Len remarks that he's glad the gig on the yacht "blew up" so they could pick up a few extra dollars back at their usual stand. He asks Brian if he's going out to Cicero to hear Benny Moten play. Brian tells him he can't make it tonight, that a friend of his, a guy who hauls freight for one of the bootleggers, has a heavy date and can't break it, and has asked Brian to pilot his truck for him. "I'll pick up twenty-five bucks, Len," Brian tells him.

Len frowns. "I wish you wouldn't hang around with those guys, Brian, they stink. Some of these days you're gonna get in hot water with them." Brian punches his brother lightly on the bicep. "C'mon, Len, don't be silly. If Shipwreck Kelly can make money sitting on flagpoles, how dangerous can driving a hooch truck be? I'll see you later."

He leaves, taking his sax case with him, and we dissolve from a close-up of Len's worried face to the alky truck, pounding down the highway, Brian behind the wheel, whistling a soft variation of "No More Saints."

Abruptly, the road ahead is filled with men and sawhorses. A barricade. In the lights of the truck we see it is Eliot Ness and several of the Untouchables; Brian panics; if he gets caught driving a load of illegal alcohol that means the end of the music, his freedom, everything. He floors the pedal and the truck leaps ahead, scattering the Untouchables as Brian crashes through the barricade. As the truck whips past, Ness and his men open up with riot guns and revolvers.

There is an agonizing moment as the truck veers crazily, spins across the road, leaps the highway and plunges off the concrete into a ditch. It runs a few hundred feet and smashes full into a telegraph pole, instantly bursting into flames. Before the Untouchables can get to the aid of the driver, the illegal alky in the truck explodes, and within instants the truck is a booming, roaring funeral pyre.

"May 30th, 1930. A routine interception of a liquor truck, resulting in the death of an obscure musician named Brian Breslin. An incident that passed from Eliot Ness's mind soon after, in the wash of more important matters, the protection of Justin Carlyle and the prosecution of 'Nucky' Johnson. But this was a death that should have been more carefully noted, for it was to become a vital piece in a puzzle of death that featured Eliot Ness and his Untouchables."

Fade out on the burning truck, flames leaping high in the night.

ACT TWO

Fade in the Chicago morgue, a slab with a sheet-covered body, a stiff manila tag tied to the large toe of the right foot. As camera angle widens, we see Len Breslin looking at the charred remains of his brother. "Okay," he says softly to the attendant, motioning vaguely with his hand for the sheet to be replaced. Rather than in words, his lost expression and the fitful movements of head and hands tells the attendant this is the deceased's brother. Len asks how it happened, and is told Brian was killed when federal men tried to stop the truck. Len wants to know which federal men and is told Eliot Ness and the Untouchables. He nods again, resignedly.

"Pick up your brother's belongings at the desk," the attendant tells Len. But Brian's possessions are reduced to one, the charred and barely-recognizable saxophone in its burned case. Len takes it, still carrying his own horn from the late-night session where he was called to come down for the identification.

Camera goes with Len as he walks the street in the chill, grey dawn of Chicago. He walks past a street corner newsstand, where the headline

D. A. CARLYLE ESCAPES DEATH

IN BOMB BLAST ABOARD YACHT

catches our eye. He walks on, and softly, we hear the melody of "No More Saints," forlorn, lost, helpless, frightened. Len Breslin has been torn in half, and that important half lies behind him on a slab in a morgue refrigerator. He walks.

Len almost unconsciously finds his way to a pawn shop as his interminable walk stretches on into the morning. In the hock shop he lays the twisted sax and his own cornet on the counter. "How much can I get on these?" he asks the proprietor. The man examines the two pieces then answers, "Ain't much good, this sax'phone, but I can give ya eighteen bucks for the trumpet." Len worries the mouthpiece of the cornet free and sticks it into his pocket. "Can I get enough on both of them for a gun?"

The proprietor looks startled, but tells him he can get a light-caliber revolver, a .22 with six bullets included. Len takes the gun and leaves the shop. The proprietor stares after him, then hangs the cornet in the window; the saxophone, with all its meaning for Len, is unceremoniously dumped in the refuse barrel as we dissolve to Len stopped on a street corner, asking a passer-by, "Is that the Federal Building?" He gets an affirmative answer and as he looks across at the building, camera cuts to his POV and we dolly in on the building, dissolving to an establishing shot in Eliot Ness's office.

Youngfellow and Rossi are slumped in chairs, looking exhausted. Ness is hanging up the phone. "What does Carlyle do, chew sugar cubes to get the energy?" Rossi remarks ruefully. "After he finished up at his office he kept going till eight this morning, from Pearley's to the 600 Club, from the 600 to Will Whittaker's speak on Division...I'll tell you Eliot, I don't know how he manages to keep going, but when we took him home this morning so he could change his clothes, he looked fresher than either of us."

Eliot smiles tightly. "He's been going like that for years."

Youngfellow chimes in, "Well, I'm glad Lee and Jack took over this morning. Let *them* get run into the pavement for a while. I want to go home and catch some sleep."

Ness vetoes his remark. "Afraid not. We have to go out to South Gary and find Wallace Pranger."

"Again? But every time we've pulled him in he swears he knows nothing, Eliot."

Ness nods. "But it's getting close to trial time, and Carlyle wants us to take another stab at it."

Youngfellow rises, commenting, "Sounds as though Carlyle may not feel he's got 'Nucky' sewed up."

Ness looks troubled; he has been driven by Carlyle's seeming verve to get Johnson. "No, the case is tight, but I think Carlyle wants every last bit of juice to get 'Nucky' convicted. Don't forget, that's a big machine we're fighting. They know we've got the goods, and they've tried every stalling technique in the books for six months to get their own case built up. They must be at a last ditch if they had to try a hit on Carlyle. And they'll probably try again."

As they leave the office, Rossi jibes, "If Carlyle's got it tied up and *he's* worried, think how our friend Enoch L. Johnson must feel."

Quick cut to the face of "Nucky" Johnson, behind wire, talking to his attorney. "Well, what did they say?" he asks. The attorney makes a noncommittal shrug. "'Nucky,' they say it's suicide trying to get Carlyle. He's got Ness and that bunch with him night and day now."

"You shouldn't have bungled it the first time out."

"'Nucky,'" the attorney whines, "this isn't taking care of some little numbers better on the South Side; this is the Prosecuting Attorney, he's a big man, with friends."

"Nucky" Johnson, simply described, looks like a dirty old man. His grey hair and jowled face give him more a look of aging decadence than dangerousness. He is a buyer, a man who possesses other men by money or service or intimidation, but never by fear and threats. Half the town is "on the pad" to "Nucky," and hence, his loyal followers are many. This has been the reason Ness has been unable to get him on a Federal charge; no one will talk. "Nucky" is liked, well-liked, and only by stumbling across the evidence of a murder, committed by "Nucky" many years before, has he been able to bring the great Soul-Buyer to task. Judges, attorneys, cops, these are only a few who are in "Nucky's" pocket.

"Well, I got friends, too, Lofting. I've got a lot of friends, and now's the time for them to do a few favors in return. I want Carlyle taken out... he's the only one could stand up to me, and they know it. Tell them I want to get out of here." Then a whining note creeps into his voice, "Lofting, you don't know what it is to be in a cell for six months...I haven't had a decent meal since I got in here...I want out...just to see a woman... feel the air rushing past my face driving in the country..." then his voice hardens again, "...I want to beat this rap, Lofting. Get them on it."

The attorney starts to gather his papers, then adds, "I still think it's a mistake to let Pranger run around loose."

"Nucky" shrugs him off. "He won't talk. He's a friend, and my friends don't cross me up, Lofting."

"I still think..."

"All right, all right, stop chattering at me. If it'll make you feel any safer in court, then get to him, I don't care, that doesn't worry me... what worries me is Carlyle...do what you like with Pranger, but make sure you do something about Carlyle, too."

Dissolve to Walter Pranger, working in a steel foundry in South Gary. He is walking down one of the aisles between the molding stools, a bucket of oil in one gloved hand, a long-handled broom for spreading the oil across the stools in the other. As he walks up the line toward the hearths, the demonic clanger of the mill pauses for an instant, as though holding its breath, and then the sound of metal pounding metal begins again.

As we move with him, we see over his shoulder, high up behind him, a stripping crane carrying a molten ingot in its mold, coming toward him. The crane is not over the stools as it should be, but over the aisle, and it moves toward Pranger steadily. Again the momentary silence, and in that instant Pranger hears the crane. He looks back over his shoulder, sees the machine coming for him, and realizes at once that it is trying to overtake him. He drops his oil bucket and swab, begins running down the aisle. The stripping crane moves more quickly on its overhead rails, and as Pranger rushes to the end of the building, begins pulling at the sidewise-sliding steel door, we see the huge, fiery ingot in its mold growing larger and larger...

Even as the stripping crane loosens its hold on ingot, mold and all, Pranger manages to slide the door open enough to worm through, and as we go with him, seeing him flatten against the other side of the door, terror large in his eyes, we hear the deafening clang of the metal hitting the place where he stood.

Pranger runs through the yard into another building, finds a telephone and dials operator. "Gimme long distance, Chicago, the Federal Building...I wanna talk to Eliot Ness..."

ACT THREE

Fade in Eliot Ness and Justin Carlyle, in shirt-sleeves, working over the pre-trial briefs. They are jubilant at Pranger's evidence. Ness comments that Johnson must be at the end of his rope if he went after Pranger at this late date, and warns Carlyle that this is only further indication that they will try to hit the D. A. before he can try the case.

Carlyle chuckles, saying it would be impossible for him to be hit by a mosquito with the Untouchables constantly breathing down his neck.

Ness concludes his work with Carlyle, tells him he is going back to his own office, and to let him know if there are further developments. Ness leaves the Court House and in a medium long shot we pan with him as he moves, then in reverse angle we see Len Breslin watching. Waiting. Deciding.

Dissolve to Len in his tiny room, later, alone, trying to plan a course of action. He removes the cornet mouthpiece from his pocket, placing the gun on the bureau, and he hunkers over the blowing-instrument tightly, blowing and humming, and we hear it is the asking-part of the tune "No More Saints."

Then, as though from some faraway land where all spoken music goes, a place where the music never dies, comes an answering melody. Faintly, then more strongly, the asking-part is answered by the melody of a saxophone. Len has reached his brother. Brian is gone, but he can still be heard. Dimly, distantly, but listening, waiting to hear what his living brother has to say.

"Brian..." he murmurs, astonishment and happiness pale in his eyes, "Brian. I saw the one who cut you off. His name is Ness. Eliot Ness, he's one of them, Brian. What can I do...I'm no good without you, no damn good at all...you saw after me for so long, Brian, I—I have to *do* something for you, I have to make it right..." he begins to cry as he returns to the mouthpiece and the ghostly two-part song. He makes his pledge in harmony, and the answer comes from nowhere, agreeing. "I'll kill him, Brian. I promise, I swear it...for you."

Slow dissolve as the music continues.

Slow dissolve as Len's small body folds into his tune.

Slow dissolve past Len to Chicago seen through the window, and

Slow dissolve to another window, and through that window to a close-up of a bottle of bootleg whiskey in a pair of hands. The bottle becomes the center of frame as camera pulls back to show us Solly Armour, the walking liquor store. He is a ferret-like little man, stubbly and dark, wearing shabby clothes and a huge, long overcoat that comes far below his knees. He now stands with the coat held open wide, revealing thirty pockets on the inside of the lining, into which bottles of whiskey are being shoved. He is the perambulating retailer of the Syndicate's booze, getting stocked up for the day's work. The woman stocking the coat is Candy Bullock, a huge Amazon of a woman, without beauty and without softness. She runs the "cordial shop" which fronts for the illegal traffic in rotgut. Several men sit around the room. As this scene has played, narration over:

"As small stores closed throughout the Depression-ridden country, their premises were immediately occupied by so-called 'cordial shops.' On their shelves they displayed bottles of 'non-alcoholic flavorings' but bootleg liquor was available from under the counters. In Chicago, this almost open and above-board system of distribution tripled the business of Enoch L. 'Nucky' Johnson, and by direct tie-up, Scarface Al Capone, America's most jovial murderer."

As the supply is being set into his coat, a phone rings o. s. and Candy takes the call. Holding her hand over the mouthpiece, she tells the two men sitting in the back room of the cordial shop, "This is what you been waiting for." She completes the call and turns to the two men. They are obviously hardcases. Barracudas, men who make their living from violence. One is cool, the other nervous, but both men are for hire. "Okay," says Candy, "that was the word. Carlyle's in his office. Which one of you's gonna drive?" One of the men nods, and Candy says to the other, the cool one, "You got all your stuff?" He acknowledges the question and they move out.

After they have gone, Solly gets stocked, leaves the back room of the cordial shop and makes for a pay phone. To call Ness. Ness listens as Solly tells him a second attempt is planned on Carlyle's life. Then he calls Carlyle.

Solly is racking the receiver and turning as he is confronted by Candy, a gun in her hand. The woman is huge, Solly is very small and frightened, suddenly. "I always wondered why you had such big ears, like a pitcher on ya, Solly," Candy says with quiet malevolence. "Who were you talking to...Carlyle's office?"

Solly does not answer as a meat-like hand reaches in from o. s. and drags him from the booth abruptly. A whiskey bottle falls from under his coat and smashes on the pavement as we cut to

Eliot Ness hurrying out of his building. So intent is he, that when he bumps into the small, dark young man he looks at him without quite comprehending what is happening.

They hang there in a moment without space or time, Eliot Ness and Len Breslin, and they stare at each other, across a space that is smaller than either knows. Then Ness mumbles an apology for his clumsiness, turns swiftly, and enters his car at the curb before Len can speak. The camera holds on Len for a beat, then the angle widens as he draws the cocked revolver from his pocket. He was ready, he was right there, ready to pull the trigger. Why hadn't he done it? Why?

He turns, spins, rushes off down the street, elbowing aside pedestrians in his hysterical confusion, his need to escape his own inability to do what must be done.

He rushes into an alley, plunges down its length and comes up short, gasping, against the brick wall, fear and humiliation in his eyes. The gun clatters to the top of a garbage can, and Len begins to writhe against the wall, his hands at his face, trying to escape his own inadequacy.

He talks to the empty air. "I could've done it, Brian. I was ready, Brian. I was right there, I was all set, but—but I wasn't, I wasn't ready for...for his eyes. *His eyes*, Brian! I had to look at him, and it wasn't that easy. I couldn't do it. You've got to understand...I tried, so help me God, Brian, I tried...but he *looked* at me, Brian.

"Brian...?"

There is no answer.

He falters, taking the mouthpiece from his pocket, and as though seeking the "Open Sesame" to the conversation, as though seeking vindication from a ghost, he begins once more to mouth the strains of "No More Saints." He plays the asking part and waits. But there is still no answer. There is no sound from the beyond. Neither from the grave nor the dark pit of his own desperate needs. Brian will not answer.

Len clutches the mouthpiece and picks up the gun. He turns and we go with him in a tight close-up as we see him nod silently, resigning himself, screwing himself to the firmness of his resolution.

"I'll go back, Brian...another time...I'll do it, please believe me, I swear I'll do it...only...*don't leave me*...please, please stay with me...I'll do it—"

Fade out on his tormented face.

ACT FOUR

The secretary outside Justin Carlyle's office barely looks up as the old man with the walrus moustache comes in. He carries a large waste basket and wears a grey service coverall. "Emptyin' the baskets, mum," he mumbles, the old pensioner picking up a few extra dollars with menial labor. The girl nods. The old man begins emptying the baskets. The girl gets up, crosses to a filing cabinet, her back to the old man, and in that instant he shambles swiftly to Carlyle's door, opens it softly, and as he passes through, straightens, pulling a heavy caliber revolver from among the refuse in his basket.

The look of age passes as he steps inside, and we see it is the cool man from the cordial shop, as he levels the gun at the startled Justin Carlyle. But even as he brings the gun into line, a pair of shots erupt from the blind corner of the room, the old man (who is not old at all) is lifted by the shock of the bullets striking, and is slammed full against the glass-window door, shattering the glass, dumping him forward in a heap, the gun unfired in his hand.

Hobson and Rossman come out from where they have been waiting, in the blind corner of the room, and Rossman stoops to turn over the body. The walrus moustache hangs crookedly off the upper lip, and Rossman pulls it away.

"Recognize him, Jack?" Hobson asks.

Before he can answer, the voice of Eliot Ness comes from the doorway. "Probably imported muscle. For a job this size they wouldn't use a local and chance getting connected."

Carlyle grins at him from behind the desk where we see he has been sitting with a gun in his lap. "Why is it you always miss the fun, Eliot?"

"Well, I won't miss any more. I'm staying with you till you walk into that courtroom tomorrow morning."

Dissolve from a close-up of Eliot Ness to

The courtroom, Cook County Court House. The room is jammed, and at one table sits Enoch Johnson, a battery of potent lawyers on either side of him, the rows behind him filled with the steely eyes and grim faces of the Syndicate and "Nucky's" friends...who have been unable to save him.

Wallace Pranger sits in that courtroom.

And at the prosecution table Chief Prosecuting Attorney Justin Carlyle—looking dapper, unruffled, seemingly untouched by the insane happenings of the past 24 hours—sits with his Assistant Counsel, the Chief of the Homicide Division of the Chicago Police, and Eliot Ness.

Ness passes the usual comments, and inevitably gets up to leave: the case is in the hands of Carlyle, his Furies, and that often-blind helpmeet, Justice.

As Ness passes through the two huge oak doors of the courtroom, into the corridor, he is suddenly stopped by the short, dark young man directly in front of him.

He looks at Len Breslin for an instant, there is a beat, a hesitant moment as the sounds of the courtroom and the gavel pounding fade away, and in that instant Len speaks one soft word, "Brian..." pulls the gun and fires at Ness.

The first shot catches Eliot in the side, spinning him with the pain. He stares at the boy uncomprehending. Then the second shot hits him. He tries to stumble away, but falls. Len does not move, but fires again and again.

Ness lies crumpled on the marble tiles of the corridor as Len drops the gun and slowly turns and walks away. Then the courtroom boils over with the mob who has heard the shots, and in the confusion, people start streaming past him from every office and courtroom, Len Breslin walks down the long corridor, cupping the mouthpiece to his lips, as the camera follows him, giving us a full-frame shot of the stately corridor. In one clump the huge ant-like crowd, with the riddled body of Eliot Ness in its center...the long white empty expanse of the corridor...at the other end, heading toward the open doors leading outside, Len Breslin, shuffling slowly, while the sound of "No More Saints" rises up and up and up, filling the whole, strange world.

Fade out.

TAG

Swift montage of scenes, as follows, while Winchell narration over:

The shriek of an ambulance as it tears away from the hospital. The ambulance weaving through traffic. Pulling up in front of the court house. Attendants rushing up the steps. Ness being lifted onto stretcher as the Untouchables stare dumbly. The ogling crowd. Pandemonium. Justin Carlyle, tight-lipped, more frightened than he has been through all of it. The ambulance screaming through the city. Cook County Hospital large in the frame. Ness being wheeled down a grim passage to surgery. The hot bank of operating lights and the face-masked surgeons sweating grayly over him. The operating theater silent but for the clack and tink of metal utensils. Ness being wheeled out of the operating stage. A surgeon saying to Hobson, "A man with luck. Few men have that kind of luck. A small-caliber weapon, amazing personal condition, no vitals were hit, we got to him in time...all of them combined, all chance, all luck. He'll live. He'll barely live." Ness broken and white in a hospital bed, and outside the window, the city; the great beast that had lain in wait for Eliot Ness, and had barely missed having him.

"May 31st, 1930; Eliot Ness lay in the hallway of the Cook County Courthouse with five bullets from a light caliber .22 revolver in him. Not quite dead, but so close that only the instant discovery of his bleeding body saved him. Ness was rushed to Cook County Hospital where he lay on an operating table for five and one-half hours. The remarkable physical condition of the man, coupled with the dark twists of Chance that had combined to save him, brought Eliot Ness back from an untimely death. On July 13th of that year, having traced the gun used on Ness, Len Breslin was arrested for Assault with Intent to Commit Murder. Except at the trial, Eliot Ness had never met the man who had sworn to kill him. How ironic it was, that Eliot Ness should escape the leveled weapons of the greatest crime Syndicate in history, only to be felled by a determined stranger, alone and unaided. So it was that the leader of the Untouchables came closest to death, by the hand of a boy who loved music and his brother and life itself, but who went to the penitentiary under sentence of life imprisonment—without ever really explaining why it was he had tried to kill a man he'd never met, Eliot Ness."

JUSTIN CARLYLE / background

Born of extremely wealthy parents in the posh Chicago suburb of Evanston, Justin Foster Carlyle spent his early years enjoying the sort of life Scott Fitzgerald would write about in THE GREAT GATSBY. A monied existence in which money was a constant, a reality, never a weapon or a conscious possession. *Noblesse oblige* was the superficial cachet used by not only Carlyle's parents, but by his entire social strata, to enjoy the status quo of silver spoons lodged firmly in mouths. Drinking was a habit Justin acquired early in life, as a party stunt for his parents—"Isn't it cute the way Jus crooks his little finger when he drinks a martini?"—along with the habit of being admired. First by his mother and older sister, his aunts, the lovely women who came to the monstrous garden parties, and inevitably the girls at the dancing academy, the pre- and post-debs he found himself dating by the age of thirteen. In 1912 Justin Carlyle was at prep school when the telegram reached the headmaster that his mother, father, and older sister had been lost when the *Titanic* sank. For some obscure reason, it was only his sister that he cried about, but with the appearance of Aunt Marguerite he settled back into the routine of getting prepared for a life of ease.

In 1917, along with a group of patriotically-fervent buddies, Justin Carlyle lied about his age and enlisted with the American Expeditionary Force. He saw France for the first time, not as an idle American touring with his parents, but as a doughboy, on June 5th, 1917 and saw fire at Aisne-Marne, Belleau Wood, in the Meuse-Argonne and Bony.

By the time he returned to the United States in January of 1919, a remarkable change had come upon Justin Carlyle; he had gained a realization of the difference between life and living. In the mud-clogged trenches of France he had seen men who wanted to get back home, for a reason; he really had no reason, no direction, no purpose. Suddenly, more than anything in the world, Jus Carlyle wanted a goal in life. Upon his return, he carefully analyzed himself, recognized the basic strengths of his nature, and almost unbidden the determination came to him to make the Law his life's work. Here was form and structure and purpose. A gestalt, a coherent rationale by which his life could gain meaning. In a burst of remarkable energy he completed Harvard Law School, won his spurs in court and climbed through a series of brilliantly-prosecuted cases from legal aid to Assistant District Attorney, to Chief Prosecuting

Attorney of Cook County. And when he had arrived, he poised on that peak and realized he had allowed his pendulum to swing too far. His life had, indeed, become the Law.

At thirty-four, Jus Carlyle had begun to separate his life into two distinct parts. His business life was an open book, a total involvement, a total commitment—a devotion to that abstract Justice that removed it from the category of cold impersonalities, made it a sentient, breathing entity. He constantly proved himself with his work. It was the sole centerpost of his life, taking the place of home and woman and family. And only at the age of thirty-four did Justin realize he had cheated himself.

So it forced back into being the other half of his life; his personal life, his social life. He began renewing atrophied friendships with the wealthy and sybaritic men and women he had renounced. The release was what he needed. The simple frenzy of parties, loud music, beautiful young women, provided an outlet, and from these two divergent segments of a life singly-directed, came the dual image of Justin Carlyle:

A dedicated man. Dedicated to something larger than fame or power or love. Dedicated to the Law, to the great monolithic entity that was Justice. A tough man with an almost pathological devotion to detail and a cunning in the courtroom that stems from his intensity with his work, he is, nonetheless, warm and easily reached. His is a combination of competence and vulnerability that women find vastly appealing. None of this warmth shows when he deals with the criminals he is sworn to prosecute. With them he is somehow on a level with them, as base and angry as they can be, as quickly moved to violence, as hag-ridden by his ethics & morality as they are by their amorality. But there is a human being underneath Carlyle's horn-hard exterior— tough, frightened, and vulnerable.

A dichotomy, an enigma, a combination of Jimmy Walker's wild, fun-loving nature and Thomas E. Dewey's rampageous determination to clean up the city. Justin Carlyle, called by his opponents "the playboy D. A." and known to his friends as very much a man. Whether it is pursuing a bottle of Bollinger '25 to its dregs, or a killer to the electric chair, Justin Carlyle's presence can be felt in all its magnetism.

He was the teeth in Eliot Ness's machinery of retribution on the Syndicate and the men who ran it.

Eight Bombs in
Search of a Target

Great Adventure (ca. 1962–1963)

FADE IN:

We are looking through a periscope at a shoreline in the dark. Through the glass, centered in the crosshairs, we see a still beach and dunes. Faintly, in the b. g. we hear the soft chug and whine of great engines, lying in wait. Then, sharply, quite loudly, one word in German is rapped out. "Auftauchen!" Surface!

SHARP CUT to water, all around us, boiling turbulent, splitting, as a great dark shape, of which we are a part, drives its way upward. Then, abruptly, the water splits on both sides, and we are free in the world.

SHARP CUT to a LONG SHOT from the beach, out to sea. A dark shape breaks the surface, water pouring from its sides, and we are staring at a U-boat. Activity begins on the deck. A rubber raft is thrown over the side, and men carrying crates bustle about. The men jump down into the boat, lines are cast off, and the men begin paddling in toward CAMERA and shore.

As this scene is being played, the following NARRATION OVER:

"The date is 12 June 1942, stated in a military manner. So stated, because four of the men in that tiny rubber boat bobbing toward the shore are soldiers. Specifically, operatives of *Abwehr* II, a division of

The German Military Intelligence Corps. *Abwehr* is a German word meaning 'defense.' But these four men are by no means on a defensive mission. The crates hulking low in the tiny raft are gorged with explosives, detonators, the raw material to blow up three hundred and seventy-two bridges...or somewhere over eight hundred troop trains... or one hundred and nineteen factories. These four men are saboteurs. They have recently completed an intensive course in the arts of mayhem, murder, demolition, and terrorism. (beat) The shore toward which they are now pulling is not European. The land in which these men plan to pass their final exams of sabotage is not a tiny principality in the path of Hitler's steel boot. (beat) It is the shore of Long Island. Just off Amagansett; and these four men have been sent from the nightmare world of the Nazis to destroy America's light metals industry. The date is 12 June 1942, and the incredible journey taken by these bombs in search of targets is a chapter of modern American history not soon to be forgotten."

As the small rubber raft beaches, and two men leap out, sub-machine guns poised, CAMERA HOLDS on the eerie tableau and we FADE OUT.

ACT ONE

FADE IN:

The beach. The rubber raft with two Nazi sailors, is departing. The four men left on the beach speak only English. One of them begins to speak in German, but the leader GEORGE JOHN DASCH snaps at him, "English! Only English!" He motions for three of them to drag the crates away in the fog. As they do, Dasch sees a light coming down the beach. He tenses and makes a move to hide; but it's too late. The light is a flashlight in the hands of a COAST GUARDSMAN. The man challenges Dasch; the German tells him he is one of several fishermen, blown off their course in the dark. The Coast Guardsman believes him, and is about to leave, when another of the men, ERNEST PETER BURGER, comes out of the dunes, still wearing his German navy outfit, and hails Dasch—in German.

Dasch reacts violently! "Shut up, you damn fool! Everything is all right. Go back to the boys and stay with them."

Burger turns without a word and returns to the other two. He tells

them to keep down, that Dasch has run into an American. The Coast
Guardsman is now nervous. A foreign language, the phrase "the boys"...
and he was unarmed. Fear.

Dasch moves toward the young Coast Guardsman.

"How old are you?" he asks.

"Twenty-one," the young man answers, nervously.

"Do you have a father?"

"Yes."

"A mother?"

"Y-yes."

"Do you want to live to see them again?"

Silence. A terrified silence of agreement.

"I wouldn't want to have to kill you."

The Coast Guardsman is rooted to the spot, terrified.

Dasch fishes in a pouch. "Here is three hundred dollars. Count it."

The Coast Guardsman hesitates. "Take it!" Dasch commands.
"Count it!" The young man does as he is told. "Now go away, and forget
about this. Or I'll find you, and I'll kill you."

The Coast Guardsman tries to move away, but Dasch grabs him by
the arm. "Wait a minute." He takes off his cap. "Take a good look at me."
The Coast Guardsman shines his light in Dasch's face.

"Look in my eyes."

Then again: "Look in my eyes; do you see that I would kill you if
you don't forget this?" The Coast Guardsman nods.

Dasch puts his hat back on. "You'll be meeting me in East Hampton
sometime. Do you know me?"

"No sir. I-I never s-saw you before in my life..."

"What is your name?" Dasch asks.

"F-Frank. Frank C-Collins," says the Coast Guardsman. He backs
up, terror on his face. Then suddenly, turns, and bolts into the fog.

The Germans bury the guns, their clothes, the bomb equipment,
their duffle, and changing to American garb, start out for the Montauk
Point station of the Long Island Railroad. It is 5:00AM.

They reach the station and wait for it to open. Meanwhile, the Coast
Guardsman has run back to the Beach Patrol station. It took him twenty
minutes to walk from the station to his meeting with the German—and
eight minutes to get back. The officer in charge at the station issues rifles
to the Coast Guardsman and three others, and the five rush back to the

spot of the encounter. Nothing. Fog. Emptiness. The Chief of the station, Warren Barnes, who had been phoned before the five men went on their search, arrives, and calls Coast Guard HQ in New York for instructions. Then he joins the men on the beach. The Coast Guardsman who met Dasch finds a pack of German cigarettes and gives them to Barnes.

Then he returns to the station; Coast Guard intelligence men are on the way. The Coast Guardsmen continue searching the beach, while just a few miles away, the Nazis wait at the train station.

Finally, the train station opens, the four men—pretending to be fishermen—buy tickets, and board the train at 6:57AM.

The express to Jamaica, Long Island arrived at 9:30 and the four men soon lost themselves in the crowd.

Meanwhile, intercut, the Coast Guard has located the buried bombs and clothing. Through channels—time-consuming channels, difficult to explain in the face of such a situation—the goods are sent to New York, and finally, the Coast Guard Intelligence calls in the FBI.

The IBMs begin to click, the analysis begins to be made, and the search is suddenly on. America has been invaded.

And while the wheels begin to turn, four deadly saboteurs walk through the crowds of New York.

FADE OUT.

ACT TWO

FADE IN:

A weather-beaten door in Amagansett. The door opens and an FBI man questions the little old lady with the dust mop: "Have you seen a man who fits this description..." and he describes Dasch. Nothing. Another door. Another question. Again, nothing. And then, a SHARP CUT to an EXT. CU of a revolver firing down a short target range at an innocuous yellow block of material. An explosion. The FBI man with the smoking revolver turning to other security men, "They have some of that explosive painted to look like chunks of coal. One piece in a train engine, a munitions plant, and the whole thing would go sky-high." Now they know they have the real thing to contend with, not merely a vague rumor.

And there is a strong possibility there may be more high explosive—

buried elsewhere, or with the saboteurs. They *must* be located immediately! And where are these men?

HEINRICH HEINCK and RICHARD QUIRIN are in a clothing store, buying new suits. They have more money than they've ever known, given to them for their expenses, and they indulge themselves. Burger and Dasch are buying, too. Like madmen. Then they go to meet their accomplices in Manhattan, at the Automat. Dasch is dismayed when Heinck and Quirin appear in loud striped sports jackets. He compliments them sardonically, but is in too much of a rush to bother telling them how to dress. He tells the men they will meet the next day, a Sunday, at a restaurant on West 52nd Street, and if they miss the rendezvous for any reason, later that day at Grant's Tomb on Riverside Drive. They split up, none of them realizing that just a few blocks east of them New York was turned out on 5th Avenue to see the "New York At War Parade."

The FBI, in the interim, was checking out the money Dasch had given the Coast Guardsman; checking banks after the money was fingerprinted. But no large transactions had been made. Another dead end. The ticket taker and the conductor on the LIRR were questioned, but to no avail.

Finally, the FBI comes to the realization that the men they are seeking are somewhere lost in the maze of New York, and that short of an unexpected break, what lays ahead is the investigation of every lead, no matter how outlandish.

And somewhere off the coast of Florida, a second U-boat is heading for shore, with a second load of four saboteurs.

Heinck and Quirin take a room at the Hotel Martinique. They go to sleep at once. It is Saturday, June 13. The next day, Sunday, the two men go to meet Dasch and Burger at the restaurant, the Swiss Chalet, but their accomplices do not show up. There is momentary panic.

There is cause for Quirin and Heinck to panic, for back in their hotel room at the Governor Clinton Hotel, Dasch has revealed to Burger that he feels their mission is doomed, that the only way they can save themselves is for Dasch to get in touch with the FBI and turn the group over. Burger agrees, saying he has been against the entire scheme from the first. Dasch decides they must keep the appointment at Grant's Tomb, to allay their accomplices' suspicions. They hurry to meet Quirin and Heinck. Dasch and Burger stall at this meeting, and there is a fight between the two factions—

Quirin and Heinck wanting to leave New York as soon as possible, to start their reign of terror—and Dasch/Burger conning them into staying.

They plan another meeting, same place, for the next day.

On the way back downtown, Dasch and Burger decide to call the New York office of the FBI, and Dasch does so, saying he is one of the Nazi saboteurs that arrived by U-boat, and that on the following Thursday he will present himself at the Washington offices of J. Edgar Hoover.

He hangs up, secure in the knowledge that he has fortified his position with the US government.

And at the other end of the line, a disbelieving FBI man looks at the slip of paper on which he has jotted Dasch's words. He chuckles, shakes his head. "Always a nut in the bunch somewhere." He throws the note into a basket labeled ROUTINE FILING.

FADE OUT.

ACT THREE

FADE IN:

A pair of hands holding cards. As we pull back we see it is Dasch, playing pinochle with friends. He is gathering courage to make the trip to Washington. Narration explains that despite his feeling the trip should be made as soon as possible, the emotional drain of having made his decision left him in need of relaxation. And from the card game, we go to Grant's Tomb again, where Burger is explaining to Quirin and Heinck that Burger is busy making arrangements and cannot meet them. The other two saboteurs are restless, frightened, they wish to take action, do something, get out of New York.

Heinck suggests they plant a bomb in a department store owned by Jews, an idea he has put forth before. He is quashed, but there is the inference that the pencil bomb in his pocket may be put to use.

On Thursday, June 18th, Dasch writes a note to Burger telling him he is going to Washington to "straighten things out." He leaves the note and boards the Washington train at Pennsylvania Station.

Burger reads the note when he returns to his room, and then goes to meet his accomplices. He tries to stall them, and they go for some relaxation, to the Swing Club. There they meet a young woman who says she can fix them up with dates the following night. On Friday night, Quirin and Heinck come to Burger's room, and while Burger is shaving, he sees in his mirror that they are searching his writing desk. They find the note from Dasch, and Burger is petrified with fear. They read it, seem disturbed, but cautious, and return it to the place it was hidden. They go out and spend the evening with the girls. At the end of the night, Quirin and Heinck leave Burger, promising to meet him the next day.

He does not know if they understood the letter, if they are planning to run off...or precisely what they have in mind. Saturday comes, and still the men say nothing, yet Burger has the feeling they are watching him.

And where is the FBI already? Surely no government agency could take so long to act on information such as Dasch's.

But Dasch could not get through to anyone in charge, in the FBI offices. He had called Army G-2 and left a message, but nothing had happened. Now again, he tried to get through, and succeeded. It was late Friday. Finally, the FBI is contacted, they tell him to remain in his hotel, and shortly thereafter, Dasch surrenders himself to the intelligence men.

He is questioned.

The pick-ups of the other seven begin. Each in turn is shown apprehended at the most commonplace of activities.

The Florida explosives are found. All eight are in custody. And now begins the incredible trial of the eight saboteurs, and the frightening climax to their long voyage.

FADE OUT.

ACT FOUR

FADE IN:

A newspaper headline: US FORCES SUFFER LOSSES IN PACIFIC.

A copy of *Life* magazine bearing the headline: THE EIGHT NAZI SABOTEURS SHOULD BE PUT TO DEATH!

A woman hanging a gold star in her window, crying, pulling the shade, a black wreath on the door.

Eight men, in American Legion uniforms, aiming their rifles at the photographer taking their picture. The reporter beside the scene says, "We'll sub-head it: Nothing less than the death penalty will satisfy

Americans—among whom are members of the Raymond Henry American Legion Post of Olyphant, Pa., who volunteered their services free as a firing squad."

All this, in sharp-cut montage; CUT TO the interior of the office of Army Colonel Kenneth Royall, defense attorney for the saboteurs. He throws down a newspaper with a glaring black headline. It's a blood-lust he senses. America is in a desperate situation on two fronts, and this is the first indication the country has had that we can cope with the twin tides of Fascism. It means a trial with the verdict a foregone conclusion.

And Roosevelt's recent order, concerning the trial, in which testimony and information not usually acceptable at trials can be admitted, makes it even more certain the eight will die.

Royall displays himself as a dedicated man who is determined that the eight shall get the same treatment any criminal in America receives.

But the tide of opinion is too strong. Bits and scenes of the trial are shown, and Dasch's motives are put in question. All eight of the men swear they only wanted to get out of their mission, that they intended no sabotage. It is patently obvious that at least six of them are lying. But Dasch and Burger have their acts to back them up.

The decision is finally handed down. Six of them die in the electric chair. Dasch and Burger go to prison, and are later released and deported.

But before the decision comes down, Royall challenges the power of the President of the United States, and the Supreme Court is called into special session, one of the three times this has happened in the history of the country.

It opens difficult and complex problems of legal jurisprudence, but eventually, the decision comes down just the same. The six die. The case is closed.

Narration tells us that this is an example of quick action on the part of the FBI, and a major victory for American democracy, for the fight of Royall was a noble one, reaching even to the highest seats of our government.

And in their separate, different ways, the heroes of the story are Dasch, the frightened little German saboteur who turned informer, and the dedicated Army Attorney who fought for them not in the name of justice, but in the name of democracy and humanity.

FADE OUT.

One Life, Furnished
in Early Poverty
Route 66 (ca. 1962–1963)

Tod and Buz are hired through Freddy Goddard, Midwest Editor of *Pixweek* magazine, an old college buddy of Tod's, to work on *Swagger* magazine, and to ferret out all the inside workings of this magazine that offers girls, drink, jazz, and hip clothes as the best of all possible lives for "the sophisticated urban male."

Buz and Tod are taken on by *Swagger's* bold young editor/publisher Simon Hale, ostensibly in the capacity of trainees for a college promotion tour, but beneath the surface is Simon's complex skein of emotional needs for an aggressive second-in-command, capable of the ruthless policies Simon fears he may not be able to continue. He singles out Buz as the likely candidate and begins wooing him with the glamorous weapons of artistic achievement, a fast-rising empire, and all the swinging good times a red-blooded tot could desire.

Tod is conservative about the scene, but Buz begins to swallow it, shell and all. Particularly when Simon insures his bet on Buz by employing Renee Martin—ex-*Swagger*mate, ex-paramour of Simon Hale, ex-officio hatchetman for Simon—as lure. For Simon knows it takes a special kind of person, a carefully-cultivated brand of ruthlessness, to keep the *Swagger* empire functioning at top-point efficiency. He tells Renee to play up to Buz, to get him involved, and to keep day-to-day reports on the victim's attitudes and desires and capacities. Renee is a ruthless barracuda, a girl who may or may not hate men, but in any event, it doesn't matter. Her actions speak louder than her motives, and after Simon has fixed Buz and Tod up, Renee takes the boys to the *Swagger* Key Club, a relatively new facet of the empire, with other clubs in New Orleans, New York, Los Angeles, and Miami. At the club Buz and Tod are subjected to another heady dose of high living, and at the same time Buz begins to learn Renee's nature; she informs him she wants all the good things in time to enjoy them, not "one life, furnished in early poverty." A late call from Simon brings Tod and Buz back to the offices of *Swagger*, where they learn the mechanics of the magazine, and Buz is even more impressed with Simon's seemingly never-waning energy.

As the days pass Buz is systematically separated from Tod, and begins to take on the superficial trappings of the *Swagger* "sophisticated urban male"—slim Italian suits, a racy patter, a certain hardness around the eyes. And he works closely with Simon, even when he is away from Simon, for Renee, as devil's advocate, begins steering his thinking the way Simon wants it. One day abroad in Chicago, Buz and Renee go to the Lincoln Park Zoo, and Buz learns of her bitterness toward men, the death of a baby, and her determination to grab all she can.

"You sound like you don't have a soul," Buz says.

Renee laughs. "My souls is like a basketball," she replies archly. "I keep it deflated in the clothes closet."

Then comes Buz's first test. Simon tells him one of his art editors has committed a serious error, costing them sales at a period when every dollar is needed, for Simon has overextended himself with the key club enterprise, and a bank note is soon coming due. He says the man must go, and he wants Buz to fire him. Tod is appalled by Buz's seeming ease in performing the hatchet job, and in Renee's presence they have an argument. Buz makes a slip about *Pixweek*, and Renee picks up on it.

While she is secretly checking it out, matters with finances get more depressing for Simon, and he decides to use a set of photos in the magazine that have been suppressed for seven years. They are shots of a present Royal Lady in a small European country, who at one time had been a Hollywood starlet, and who had allowed a series of provocative shots to be taken while she was still struggling. Now, seven years later, they would unquestionably destroy the royal marriage and cause serious repercussions. But they would build circulation. Simon decides to use the photos, despite Tod's objections that they will be harmful; Buz and Tod once more come to harsh words over it.

"You mean you *really* don't see anything wrong in running those shots?" Tod asks Buz.

Buz shrugs. "She took them; she should have thought of it when she was posing. It's not our responsibility."

"So this is an example of the uplifting quality of material this magazine pushes, is it?" Tod snaps.

"It's circulation," Buz passes it off.

Tod looks at Buz with disapproval and disgust. "Man, you are really Simon Hale's pistolero. I didn't think anyone could go this sour, this quickly. But you've been working at it with both barrels."

Buz flares up. "Don't get sanctimonious with me, Tod. We've been rolling around for a long time now, looking for the answers. Well, I think I've found them here. Simon has something hot, and he wants me to help him keep it hot. So if it takes a little submerging of the niceties, well, I can handle that part of it."

Renee finds out about *Pixweek*, but does not tell Simon. She keeps the information for future use. Meanwhile, Simon Hale is in immediate trouble. The note is coming due, and he has to find a way to stall it till the sales jump from the controversial photos. He decides to use collusion, the badger game, to ensnare the banker intent on collecting. He throws a yacht party in the Chicago boat basin, and gets one of his loyal ex-*Swagger*mates to make a play for the married banker. The girl feigns drunkenness, and asks the banker to take her home. With half a dozen other people, including Buz, they go to the girl's apartment, and the banker, by secret agreement among the people, takes her upstairs. Then everyone leaves, except Buz, who waits to take the man home.

But as far as everyone is concerned, the man did not come downstairs again. Buz knows he did, but Simon has no reason to expect Buz will not fall in with his scheme.

When Simon springs his blackmail trap on the banker, the man comes to Buz for the backing he needs to get the truth known. Buz is in a quandary. If he backs the banker, Simon will toss him out; if he goes with Simon he is ruining an innocent man's life.

Buz turns to Renee for advice.

She tells him to swing with Simon, that it will be better for him in the long run. But Buz has not been that completely corrupted yet; he tells Tod what has happened, and they decide that now is the time to pull out of the *Swagger* empire, get back to *Pixweek* and report their findings, including the blackmailing of the banker.

Simon, overwhelmed with pleasure at his coup, has called another get-together, at his fabulous Shore Drive home, and at the party Buz puts the screws to Simon: let the banker off the hook, and they won't include it in their article. Simon realizes the ruthlessness he has taught Buz is now being employed against him. He acquiesces with anger, and in a spurt of fury swings on Buz. Buz floors him and the two boys leave Simon's house.

Renee helps Simon to his feet, and reveals that she knew all along the two boys were spying for *Pixweek*. Simon grabs her, demands to know why she didn't let him know sooner, instead of letting him put his plans in jeopardy by trusting a man who had not been completely won to their cause. She smiles, the barracuda at last revealing her teeth, and says, "Simon, you don't know it, but you've got a new partner. A very hungry partner. They may not say everything about this affair, but I'm the only other one who knows, and if I don't start becoming important around here, who knows, you might be back doing copywriting for that mail order house."

The two wild animals will fight among themselves, will inevitably destroy each other, for evil cannot feed off evil without gorging itself.

Simon, trapped by his own machinations, runs out of the house to hurl final insults at Buz and Tod.

"You'll never work in the magazine field again! I'll see that *Swagger* kills you...don't worry, I've got the power...I've got the power to smother you...you've got as much chance as a snail in a bucket of salt!"

Buz, grinning, slides up on the tonneau of the Corvette as it starts to move. "Hey, Publisher," he shouts to Simon Hale, "cancel my subscription!"

The Corvette burns rubber, away from Simon Hale and his tottering empire.

NOTE: preceding is the script as intended for development. Following is a discarded first draft, plot inadequate, but containing important characterization and additional scenes to be inserted in the revised version.

Please view as intended.

FADE IN:

CLOSE-UP of a pair of socked feet, crossed neatly on a desk. As the CAMERA, PULLS BACK and ANGLE WIDENS we look up the slim body of Freddy Goddard, Midwestern Editor for *Pixweek* magazine. He is a very proper Madison Avenue-type, despite exile in the mid-continent from which his news and photos emanate. His hair is cut short and flat, his expression is a courtesy extended between the hours of nine and five, his clothes are reserved and only slightly more apparent than JFK's two-button uniform. There is a faint aura of boredom about him, as though all the years at prep school and Yale, all the nights spent at coming-out parties and beer-tipples at the Hasty Pudding Club have prepared him for a more languid life than hustling contemporary events for America's top newsmagazine. But despite his highly contemporary demeanor, Goddard has the twinkle of a latent bohemian—the naked socks give a hint of that. This is a man capable of pulling Brooks-attired rabbits from hats.

"But why us?"

The speaker is Tod Stiles, seated beside Buz Murdock on the other side of Freddy Goddard's desk. "Why pick us? Spying isn't really our line, y'know."

"Yeah," Buz chimes in, "you must have a hundred guys around here who can do the job."

Goddard scratches the sole of one foot. "I didn't trace you two down all over the countryside just for giggles. Three good reasons, *very* good reasons, why you're ideal for this assignment.

"In the first place, *Pixweek* has a dozen regional offices, and this is one of the least important. Not that much news is made out here. So I have to scrounge for copy. When I can *make* it, I'm ahead of the game. So I dreamed up this idea of examining the *Swagger* Magazine empire, and I don't want the other bureaus in on it, stealing my thunder."

"Well, I don't know, Freddy, it's been a long time since I've done any writing—" Tod says.

Goddard waves away his objection with an imperious gesture. "Pfoo! When you were working under me on the *Record*, you were the best columnist Yale ever had. So I know you can write the piece."

"What's the third reason?" Buz asks.

"You two are perfect for the assignment. I want to find out everything about *Swagger* magazine and its subsidiary activities: the key clubs, the products with the *Swagger* stag-head on them, the whole empire...and you two are very much contemporary with the image *Swagger* offers as 'the sophisticated urban male.' You don't have any preconceived ideas about it, and what's best of all, they don't know you over there. They'll never suspect you're doing a spade job from the inside."

Tod bites his lip, shakes his head. "I don't know, Freddy. When we got the wire I was intrigued, of course, but, well, we try to keep on the move, and this thing looks to be a full-time career..."

Goddard takes a magazine from a stack on his desk and tosses it to Tod. "Here's the area you'll be working in," he says.

Tod opens it, and a gatefold of a gorgeous girl unfolds itself. Buz gives a long, lean whistle. They flip through the magazine, noting the emphasis on girls, fast cars, girls, good food and drink, girls, high living. "Let's not be too hasty, Tod..." Buz suggests.

Tod begins to grin broadly. "You mean it's true? This is the kind of life they lead over there *all* the time?"

Goddard spreads his hands. "That's what I want you to find out. I think there's something important happening and I want to know what it is. I think we can say something definitive about the status thing...or perhaps even find out if this dream-image *Swagger* offers is legitimate."

Tod and Buz look at each other, a bit sheepishly, for it is obvious their decision is being influenced more by the glamour shown in the magazine than in the lofty moralities Freddy Goddard is discussing.

"How will you get us in?" Tod asks.

"I've arranged with Simon Hale for your jobs over at the *Swagger* offices. They do a big college tie-in every year, and use young guys like yourselves to keep tabs on campus fads, styles, interests. And they help set up *Swagger* parties at fraternities. There's a six-week training program and indoctrination. That ought to be time enough for you to get the meat of the operation. Well, what's your answer? I've got a pair of second-stringers in mind if you don't want it."

"And we get paid for this?'" Buz asks.

Goddard nods. "Double. Simon Hale pays, too, while you're training."

Buz looks at Tod, Tod looks at Buz. They both look at the magazine. "We'll take it," Tod says.

CUT TO:

Buz and Tod closing the door of Goddard's office. They stand in front of the legend FREDERICK F. GODDARD, MIDWEST EDITOR, PIXWEEK for a long moment, grinning at each other. Then Buz chuckles roguishly, "Ring-a-ding-ding!" and they move rapidly away on either side as

CAMERA COMES IN TIGHT ON DOOR AND

TITLE ZOOMS IN:

ONE LIFE, FURNISHED IN EARLY POVERTY

ACT ONE

FADE IN:

MED LONG SHOT street, day, the face of a converted brownstone building, remodeled into a very dramatic office complex. The face of the building is clean and spartan, with contrasting drapes of solid hue in the windows. A pair of large glass doors dominate the platform at the top of a short, wide flight of stairs. There are no signs or names on the structure, save over the door, on the blank face of the stone, a huge stylized STAG'S HEAD, symbol of SWAGGER MAGAZINE.

CAMERA MOVES IN SLOWLY AS

Corvette pulls up at the curb in front of the building.

CAMERA CONTINUES TO MOVE IN ON BUZ AND TOD IN CAR

AS TITLE ZOOMS IN:

ONE LIFE, FURNISHED IN EARLY POVERTY

CAMERA HALTS WITH CLOSE SHOT of back of Tod and Buz's heads, as we see—between them and over their shoulders—the glass doors part and a pair of slim, sleek, well-fed girls rotate down the steps. One carries a large hat-box, and the other's hair is a phantasmagoric bouffant only slightly less imposing than Grand Canyon at dawn. They are both exquisite. Buz and Tod are out of focus as they come down the steps, toward the car, and then leave off-camera left as the glass doors part again, and a third girl, devastatingly beautiful, fantastically-cantilevered, and vibrant, comes through in a clip-clop of spike heels and swirling blonde ponytail.

She comes toward the car, then leaves off-camera right as BUZ AND TOD COME INTO FOCUS.

"This must be the place," Buz jibes, and Tod turns toward the camera to grin back impishly. They ogle each other in a broad low-comedy manner, and then Tod opens his door, getting out onto the sidewalk, as Buz shoves himself up and out over the side of the car.

CAMERA PULLS BACK AS

Buz and Tod start across the sidewalk to the building. As they mount the steps, the CAMERA ZOOMS IN ON THEM, and HOLDS as they push open the doors, one on each glass side, wide, and enter the building.

They mount a second short flight of stairs, passed by another pair of svelte, attractive girls in tight skirts, at whose passage they turn to stare. Then they mount the stairs and approach the reception desk.

Behind the reception desk is a glass case, the contents of which are *Swagger* products: a set of panties (one for each day of the week) with the *Swagger* stag head embroidered on one leg; several books, THE BEST STORIES FROM SWAGGER, RIBALD HUMOR FROM SWAGGER, and GREAT CARTOONS FROM SWAGGER; several cocktail glasses, stag-emblazoned; a *Swagger* party kit; a *Swagger* calendar with fold-out girls, etc.

Also behind the reception desk is a luscious redhead, hair teased and ratted into a monumental bubble hairdo. Her eyes are dark and sensual with makeup. She is poring over a Rolodex card file, and trying to talk into the phone which rests against her shoulder in a plastic cradle, while scribbling something on a *Swagger*pad. She murmurs acknowledgment into the phone, racks it, and turns to Buz and Tod who are shamelessly staring down her cleavage.

"May I help you?" she says, turning a calculated-to-the-kilowatt smile on them. She might as well have been saying *coffee, tea, or milk?* It's the same vacuity.

"We have an appointment with Mr. Hale," Tod says. "He's expecting us." The girl's expression becomes more interested; these two obviously have status. She smiles, and picks up the intercom phone, asking them to wait one moment. She speaks into the receiver, then cradles the phone and—with blatant sexuality, a definite come-on—advises them, "The elevator, fourth floor."

Tod moves away to the elevator, pushes the button, then goes back and retrieves Buz, still grinning idiotically at the now-openly-flirting receptionist.

Inside the elevator, Tod presses the button labeled "4" and as they rise, Buz says, "I think *Pixweek* is trying to find monsters where there are only bunny rabbits."

Tod looks at him gravely. "Correction: stags."

"All right, stags, then. Either way, this doesn't look like the den of iniquity Goddard hinted at."

"It's certainly sensational enough," Tod replies.

Buz shrugs. "Okay, sure. Sensational. A horde of good-looking girls is by definition sensational. But that doesn't call for slanted stories."

"Who says we'll slant?"

Buz grins. "I will. The other direction."

Tod shakes his head in helpless good humor. Irrepressible Buz. The elevator doors open. The fourth floor is a paneled waiting-room, with another Circe behind a clean and shining desk. "Mr. Stiles; Mr. Murdock?" she asks, even before they have left the elevator.

"I'm Stiles," Tod says, "he's Murdock."

"Follow me, won't you please," and the girl rises, leading them through a door and down a long corridor between un-officed work areas in which dozens of dapper young men pore over galley sheets, reams of copy, slide 35mm photo projectors and typewriters. There is a cricket-like hum of activity from everywhere, and Buz and Tod note it in passing. It is not all play at *Swagger*, to be sure.

As they pass through the bullpen area of underling editors, they turn left into a cross-corridor, dark-paneled and quiet. The walls are evenly-spaced by framed gatefold girls from *Swagger*, and as BUZ AND TOD WALK DOWN HALL

CAMERA CUTS TO PICTURE OF GIRL

CUTS BACK TO BUZ'S FACE, appreciative

CUTS TO ANOTHER PICTURE

CUTS BACK TO TOD, bemused and interested

CUTS TO PICTURE

CUTS TO ANOTHER PICTURE

CUTS TO CLOSED DOOR, THROWN OPEN SUDDENLY

To look through the doorway, in Buz and Tod's POV, we get our first glimpse of Simon Hale, the dynamic young publisher who has created a multi-million dollar operation from the fertile contents of his sophisticated, urban mind.

Hale is a tall, slim man in his late thirties, hair cut in a simulated Peter Gunn effect, lean face capable of limited expression, but eyes fiercely alert and somehow systemically tuned to the movements of his long, slim fingers. There is something dark, wolfish about him, though masculine, mannered, and even possibly handsome. He is at one and the same time a woman's sort of man, and very much a man's man. His voice is controlled, yet with a rising current of enthusiasm and excitement. He is directing his attentions to several extremely large press sheets, from the roto colorpresses, and accenting his discourse with the two art directors by slashing and sometimes circular movements with a red grease pencil.

"The yellow is out of register...here...here...and here," he circles the offensive areas quickly. "They brought up the red nicely in this roast beef shot, Timmy, but they overcompensated all across the roller, and we've got a sunburned look on the *Swagger*mate. Have them tone this flesh down about ten, no, fifteen per cent...and get that yellow back in register."

He pauses in the running commentary to note Tod and Buz standing in the doorway. "Stiles? Murdock? Be with you in a minute." He doesn't wait for their reply, goes back to his two assistants and a fresh press sheet.

"Timmy, too much bottom here. This girl isn't a carhop, she's a Hollywood hopeful we convinced to pose for the book. She's got to be shown a little more decorum. Have Vince scrap this shot..." he X's it out ruthlessly, just a note of annoyance in his voice, "... and substitute the bikini shot at Malibu. We've got to get a little respectability into this, even if it *is* a zilch feature. Don't sweat it, we've still got the front spread and the *Swagger*mate. Okay?" he grins, again does not wait for affirmation, adds, "Okay."

The two art assistants propel themselves from the office through another door. They go like puffed rice, shot from guns.

Simon Hale's gaze rises to the two boys and a fifty megaton explosion of charm and *bonhomie* hits them. This is a man capable of evoking absolute dedication from his co-workers, and awe in passersby whether they know his achievements or not. He is a man of personality and obvious conviction. He extends a hand as though it were a scepter. "Stiles."

Tod steps forward as though commanded, and shakes Simon Hale's hand. The grip is imperative, memorable. "And Buz Murdock..." the same treatment. He waves them to low, impressive Eames chairs, and perches himself on the edge of the cluttered work-desk, shoving aside stacks of papers and a light-box for viewing color transparencies.

"So you're friends of Irv Kupcinet," he begins. "Well, Irv's done us some good favors with his column, and if you've got the stuff to swing with *Swagger*, then I won't be doing him a favor at all." He has laid it all on the line in a few words, and incidentally told Buz and Tod how Freddy Goddard arranged their jobs: through the well-known Chicago columnist, Irv Kupcinet.

"Well, we'll do our best, Mr. Hale," Tod ventures.

Hale purses his lips and nods with satisfaction. "Good enough. Now, you understand our training program, and what we'll want you to do once you're on the road for us. A substantial percentage of our circulation is in and around colleges, so we try and keep as tight with the collegiate scene as possible. You'll be our road representatives in certain places, helping them coordinate *Swagger* parties at fraternities, setting up fashion displays in campus shops, keeping us informed of the latest trends and interests of the college kids..." he pauses.

"I think you boys will fit in just nicely here. Irv gave you a healthy recommendation."

Before Tod or Buz can answer, the intercom bleats and Simon Hale twists his body sidewise on the desk to flip up the toggle. "Uh-huh?" he asks.

A barely recognizable burst of words, obviously angry, erupts from the mechanism. Simon Hale's face breaks into an infectious grin and he cuts in to say sharply, "All right, Ray, all right, I'll be right in. Hold them there till I get over."

He flips off the intercom and stands. "I'll have to cut it short today. I was hoping we'd be able to take a quick walkthrough of the building, just to get you oriented, but that was my senior editor with a problem. Look, why don't you come over to the club tonight, I'll have a pair of *Swagger*mates for you, to keep you busy, relax a little this evening, then tomorrow we can start knuckling you down."

"What club?" Buz asks, as they rise, as Hale shows them to the door.

"The *Swagger* Key Club. This one is the first we opened, but we have them in New Orleans, Miami Beach, and three more opening next year. I think you'll like it."

"See you at eight thirty," Hale adds, shakes their hands and hustles them out into the corridor, without the slightest trace of bad manners or sloughing-off.

CUT TO:

(Repetition of shots that ended Teaser)

Buz and Tod closing the door of Simon Hale's office. They stand in front of the blank, expensive wood for a long moment, staring at each other with stunned expressions. Hale is the very apotheosis of dynamism in the young executive cloth. He is a man both can envy. But there is a definite distinction between the expressions on Buz and Tod's faces:

BUZ is aglow with the glamour and excitement of a rising American enterprise built on the glitteriest of *dolce vitas*. He looks at Tod with satisfaction and smugness.

TOD looks back with a faint shine of disturbance in his eyes. He makes a small moue with his lips and gives a noncommittal shrug. He'll wait to see how things work out.

They move off-camera and we

SHARP CUT TO

Inside of SWAGGER KEY CLUB: looking down central dining area toward a table behind which are seated Tod, Buz, and two girls, CAMERA POV:

A sumptuous, almost-palatial scene of grandeur. Along the right wall an ornate mahogany bar, saved from decay in a modish hotel of the Gold Coast days, is racked with well-dressed young men and their girls. Perched on plush stools they exchange smiles, laughter and strenuous gaiety, matching the joviality of the four bartenders in elaborate Gay Nineties bowlers and red velvet vests who serve up the drinks with both hands. The backbar mirror is elaborate, the walls are crimson velvet, and through the tables weave exquisite *Swagger*mates with sexily-cut costumes, dispensing succor and liquor.

CAMERA DOLLIES IN

Catching here and there a scene of splendor

(A free lunch counter heaped with chicken, roast beef, corned beef, and other delicacies in overflowing plates.)

(A beefy customer with his arm thrown about the bare waist of one of the serving girls, whose head is thrown back in laughter while she awkwardly tries to fend him off.)

(A rinky-tink piano, played by a gremlin of a man in galluses and bowler and checkered vest, with five or six customers singing-along as they lock arm in arm.)

(A customer peeling half a dozen bills off his roll to pay his tab.)

DOLLY IN TO MEDIUM CLOSE-UP OF

Buz with Renee, Tod with Budgie, behind a table gay with paraphernalia of *Swagger* (cocktail glasses, swizzle sticks, small bangers for hitting rhythm on glass when pianist is playing, cigarettes, et al.). They are clumped together naturally, but in groups of two, with the guys paying close attention to their dates.

TWO SHOT OF Buz and Renee as Buz says, "Want another?"

Renee is a lovely girl with dark hair caught up in one of the elaborate contemporary styles; her eyes are dark and her mouth full. On first look, she could be just another of the sex objects men admire for looks, but nothing more. She *could* be, except that as the CAMERA SWITCHES TO CLOSE-UP OF RENEE we see there is native intelligence and character in her face. There are tension lines about the eyes, the mouth. She has a restless nervous quality underlying the beauty, and the ability to strike quickly with humor or sarcasm. She is not a dumbbell.

She puts her hand over her glass. "Not just now, Buz, thanks." She looks worried. CAMERA CUTS TO TWO-SHOT OF Tod and Budgie.

Budgie is precisely what Renee is not. She is a good time girl with a head stuffed full of used Kleenex. Her eyes are wide and bright and her expression is one of sensual naïveté. She is a *Swagger*mate and no more. She will consider the loftiest ambition a full-length Emba Cerulean mink that she can drag behind her, across the deep pile rug in her apartment. Then she will know she is living. She is very definitely *not* Tod's type, but for chuckles, she is very well-built and many laughs.

They exchange pleasant banter, enough to tell us Tod is digging facts about *Swagger*mates from her nearly-empty head. CAMERA CUTS BACK TO Buz and Renee.

"You can't get much for a penny these days, but that's supposed to be the going rate for thoughts. You look like you have something bothering you. Have I got bad breath?"

She smiles wanly and touches his hand with reassurance. "No, Buz, it isn't you. In fact, after some of the King Kongs I've been saddled with, you're a gem."

Buz begins to draw her out, discovers that though she seems to be a real swinger—anything for a kick!—there is a mask of smiles drawn across sadness. He begins to talk to her more closely, as though his interest is getting aroused. The scene in the key club swirls between utter abandon and serious undercurrents of Renee's life, as she dodges most of Buz's questions, yet explains herself in broad strokes. Buz finds himself deeply attracted to the girl, and Tod notices with a disquieted air. Buz seems to really be throwing himself into the scene with both feet.

A call is paged through the club for Mr. Stiles & Mr. Murdock. Tod takes the call. It is Simon Hale. He wants them to come over to the *Swagger* offices, at once. Tod says, "Now? But it's almost midnight. We thought you were coming over here."

Hale raps out a second request that they make it over at once; the offices are a few blocks away. Tod says he'll get Buz and be there in fifteen minutes.

When they arrive, puzzled, they find the entire building dark, save for Simon Hale's office, from which window a blaze of worklights blaze out into the empty street.

They find Hale, and he sweeps them up with his urgent laying-out of the magazine's enterprises, telling them that he goes without sleep for one night each week, thus picking up an extra day of work. His electric personality and sure deft touch with the most complex problems awes Buz, and Tod too feels a certain respect for the man. Hale leads them on a tour of the offices where he personally checks everyone else's work, and they sit in on a high-level phone conversation with the possible manager of a Denver *Swagger* key club. Hale talks to them, tells them he is looking for bright young men to take high echelon positions in the staff.

"When I started this magazine, eight years ago, I was only twenty-six. I was still in touch with my generation. Not that I've gotten out of touch, you understand, but the essence of this concept, the *Swagger* concept, is that it's a sounding-board for the bright young urban male. Eight years can remove you in small ways, from the people you want to reach, the generation growing up to take their place. I need someone to set these fine points straight. You two are projecting what we like to call 'a very contemporary image' and if you click here, there might be more than just a road job with *Swagger*."

Buz beams and Tod acknowledges the offer with reservation. Hale tells them they should get back to their dates now, and he dashes off to do more work as Buz and Tod leave the building. Outside, in the quiet Chicago street, Buz speaks of Hale with near-reverence, saying there's a chance here to find Xanadu, the golden land. A life of productivity and a swinging good time, watching a worthwhile publishing venture expand, and being an integral part of it.

Tod is more reserved. He says all that glitters might not even be iron pyrites. He advises Buz to be cautious. Buz pooh-poohs the words of warning, and they return to the club to rejoin their dates.

Renee tells Buz she has to get home, and Tod says he'll stay at the key club with Budgie till Buz gets back. Buz and Renee drive to her apartment, and as they drive, Buz tells her how enthused he is about the scene. Renee tries to tell him something, but the words refuse to come out in a manner that will give Buz a definite idea of her opinion of *Swagger* and Simon Hale.

They go upstairs, and she gives Buz her key, to open the door. Buz is inclined to think he might score, but as he's unlocking the door, Renee tip-toes across the hall and knocks on another door. As Buz watches, the door opens, a pair of arms hand out a soft, warm bundle, and Renee comes back to her own door with an armload of baby.

She kisses Buz goodnight on the cheek, takes her keys, and goes inside. For the third time that day, CAMERA DOLLIES IN FOR EXTREME CLOSE-UP

As Buz realizes there are wheels within wheels in even the most simple-looking situations. The swingingest thing since sliced bread is Renee, but she's got a baby.

What the hell is her story?

ACT TWO

FADE IN:

As the days pass scenes are interspersed between Simon Hale's dynamic personality, and Renee's growing attachment with Buz. Tod begins to compile his information at last, and Buz, looking over his shoulder, is annoyed and angry that Tod seems to feel there is a subtle decadence in the *Swagger* concept, in the image the magazine is selling "the urban male," and in the dead-end life a guy begins to lead. He tells Tod he thinks there is sour grapes involved, that he, Buz, finds the *Swagger* existence a rich and fulfilling one.

Tod warns him that there is a kind of creeping moral paralysis involved, that just on the most basic of levels, mechanically, the human body can't stand up to the kind of wild partying and sybaritic life Simon Hale offers as "the good life." And he warns him about Renee, saying she is a trouble chick. Buz flares up, calls Tod a latent Puritan and unable to really relax. He says he is considering taking Hale's now-firmed offer of steady employment with *Swagger*. Tod flares back, and they come to blows.

Buz knocks Tod to the floor and stalks out of their motel room. He goes looking for Renee.

DISSOLVE TO

Renee standing in front of Simon Hale's desk, as Hale tells her she must go to work in the new Denver *Swagger* key club. Renee argues, telling him she has a baby, that she can't go to work as one of the *Swagger*mates in the club, that it's a stinking job and she doesn't want her daughter to grow up knowing her mother spends her nights getting her bottom pinched. Hale uses his big guns, telling her she is under contract to *Swagger*, that he will toss her out on her ear if she doesn't come through. She insists she wants to keep working as she has, around the *Swagger* offices, doing mail order work, and Hale tells her they are overstocked with cute types who like to pound typewriters, that she can't even take dictation, and that one of the big status things in the key clubs, that is making them successful, is the use of Ex-*Swagger*mates as cocktail waitresses. He tells her he'll expect her answer soon.

She leaves as Buz arrives, and she brushes by him trying to keep from bursting into tears. He is confused, but goes in to see Simon, to ask him what the trouble is with her.

Simon comes on strong with Buz, saying he feels he is better-adjusted for a position with *Swagger* than Tod, that Tod seems somehow to look with disdain on the operation.

Buz, caught up with fury at Tod's position, and by the peculiar brushoff Renee has given him, decides one sure way to get in with Simon Hale is to fink on Tod. He tells Simon Hale he respects him, and wants to make it with *Swagger*, and to prove his loyalty, he reveals what Tod and himself were assigned to do. Hale is concerned, but conceals his anger. He tells Buz he appreciates what he has done, that indeed he *does* admire Buz, and wants him as a high-echelon official on the *Swagger* scene.

He tells him he is having a party that night at his home, and wants Buz to get Tod to come.

Buz leaves, and outside the office is accosted by one of the secretaries who says, "You look like a guy who's just got turned down for a raise."

"No, as a matter of fact I got the raise," Buz says, sadly. "Thirty pieces of silver."

ACT THREE

FADE IN:

The party. Sodom was a Mormon picnic by comparison. A swimming pool in the center of the living room. Chicks in rhinestone-studded bikinis, stingers in hand, platinum hair coiffed to enchant, dominate the scene. Hungry-eyed guys bounce off the walls, their hands here and there on soft flesh, their thoughts in the bedrooms, their minds aswim with the importance of their place in the sun, their absolute hipness. Good jazz lays a sound-pattern across the crowd noise, the rising peaks of shrieked laughter, the susurration of gossip and liaison melting through the haze of alcohol and smoke. It is a tapestry from THE CANTERBURY TALES, a bit of society plucked free and set down in all its facets. Against this microcosm is played the final resolution of Buz's struggle to find his star.

Tod takes Renee aside, gets from her the story of her trouble with Simon Hale, tells her Buz is ruining himself under the misapprehension that he has found Valhalla. She says she has grown very fond of Buz, too fond perhaps, and she will try to do something about him.

Buz comes back to her and takes her aside himself, tells her he has decided to accept Simon Hale's offer, and that he has revealed to Simon that he and Buz were spies for *Pixweek*. She is appalled at his turncoat treatment of Tod and tells him so. He grabs her by the arms and puts her in a corner, telling her, "Look, I've been running all my life. I've got a backtrail of traveling that'd go twice around the moon. I'm tired of fast-stepping, and this is the way I've always dreamed of living. I haven't got anything much yet, Renee, and I can't talk about marriage or kids and houses with ivy on them, but there's room on Simon's ladder for me, and if you can stick around a while, we might be able to do that thing." She laughs at him. She sneers and says, "Simon's ladder? Simon's garbage hole, you mean. I'll show you how rich and worthy Simon's mud puddle can be. Come on."

She takes him by the hand, over to Simon, who is engaged in talking over a possible filming of his life story with a top Hollywood star, and she breaks in on his conversation.

"Simon," she badgers him, "I've decided not to take that B-girl job in the Denver club."

"Talk to me later, Renee," he dismisses her, "I'm discussing something important right now."

"What's the matter, Simon, don't you want the world to know all isn't sweetness and light in the *Swagger* empire?"

"I said later, Renee." He is annoyed, but turns his back to her.

"You want me to farm out my daughter to a nanny, Simon? You want me to show my skin to the big spenders in Denver? What if I don't go, Simon? What then?"

"Contract, baby," he snaps, angrily, a tinge of crimson showing through his composure. "Contract. Body and soul to me, for two years."

"The merry-go-round isn't worth it, Simon. I'm tired of having people look at me and see measurements, not a human being. It stinks, Simon, the whole gig."

Simon whirls on her. "Say, who the blazes do you think you are, you stupid bit of fluff? I made you someone to look at. I had your shape on every barracks wall and fraternity locker in the country for thirty days. I made you the only thing you'll ever be...a sex symbol for two million guys. So don't jump salty with me or I'll have you in the dust bin by morning."

Buz steps in. "Hey, Simon, take it easy. Don't talk to her like that."

Simon is enraged, the veneer gone. The monomaniacal understructure apparent now. "And you stay out of it, boy. You and that Quisling you hang with. You're both on the way out. I'm just trying to figure what action I can take against you legally for trying to subvert my staff and spread libel."

Tod backs Buz. "Get off the dreamboat, Simon. You're just the first guy to build an empire on vicarious sex. The literary pretensions wear thin this late at night."

Simon flips. "You!" he points a finger at Renee. "You're on your way to Denver, and I'm going to make sure they keep your frame real busy, extra specially busy. And as for you two, get the devil out of my house. I've got the answer to what smart guys want, and I don't need you or that fink Goddard to muddy the waters."

Tod snarls back, "Phoney dreams, Simon. A whole world of phoney dreams. But pretty quick you're going to get short of wind, and the swinging will come to a screeching halt. And then you'll be tired, Simon, very tired of it, and so will the two million suckers you delude every month with this sixteen pounds of dogmeat you call urban and sophisticated."

"Ingrate!" Simon spits, and swings on Tod.

Buz steps in and decks Simon with one punch.

On the street, in front of the Corvette, Tod and Buz look at Renee. Buz says to her that it doesn't have to end for them. She kisses him gently and tells him she has a baby to bring up, that she has to retrace her steps and find out where she substituted fear for living. She says she'll go it on her own for a while, but that they're bound to be traveling the same road again some day.

She walks up the street, away from them, and Buz looks at Tod sheepishly. "How many ways can you say 'I told you so'?"

Tod grins. "Consider them said."

"Wow, what a long dream *this* has been!" Buz sighs wearily. They move to get into the Corvette. As they start the engine, the door of Simon Hale's house bursts open, and Simon, holding a hankie to his bleeding nose, comes racing out, to stand in a pathetic mock-arrogant pose. He makes wild, wide gestures at the boys.

"I'll get you hung wherever you go!" he shouts. "I'll sue the shirts off you and that magazine if you write anything about us! I'll see you never work again! You'll never swing for *Swagger!*"

Buz slides up onto the tonneau of the Corvette and cups his hands to his mouth. "Hey, Tycoon," he shouts, "cancel my subscription!"

The Corvette burns rubber away from the curb and the

CAMERA PULLS BACK as the Corvette speeds smaller and smaller down the street, until we

FADE OUT.

The Girl in the
Spinning Glass Globe
Route 66 (ca. 1962–1963)

Joanna was brought over from Brighton by KLM, under contract to the Loesser family, to play nana to the three kids, to cook and clean and wash. Status—the snob appeal of the *nouveau-riche*, a walking reality in the person of an attractive young English or Swedish girl who will serve the family. And if anything, Joanna is *too* attractive.

But after ten weeks as a drudge, suffering the unwanted attentions of the master of the house, after suffering ten weeks of pinched behinds and distasteful scuffles in the pantry, Joanna runs off from the family, and to pay her debt to the airline, gets a job as cocktail waitress and cigarette girl in the newly-opened Millionaire's Club, on Restaurant Row in Hollywood.

Hired as a "ball girl," one of several beautiful young women who sit in the huge revolving ballroom globe that spins in the foyer of the Club, Joanna meets Tod. Killing time in Los Angeles till Buz is released from the hospital, Tod has applied through a newspaper advertisement for a position with the Club. Having fulfilled the requirements of "personable young man, college graduate, well-built, to serve as Assistant Floor Manager of fabulous new glamour restaurant and health club," Tod has been hired as general trouble-shooter for the Club; he works with three "security police" who are LA police during daylight hours, but who pick up twice their weekly police paychecks by "moonlighting" as security/muscle after hours.

As the show opens, Tod is passing Joanna in the main showroom of the Club. She has a cigarette tray across her shoulders and they exchange pleasantries. At that moment, the Manager of the Club comes up and smiles at Joanna. It is obvious she is a well-adjusted, thoroughly likeable girl whose pleasant air engages everyone. The Manager tells her they are adding a new sideline to the ciggy trays, and proceeds to put several baby dolls into her tray.

Joanna's eyes widen, and she screams in panic, hurling the tray from her, and crashes into patrons in her frantic flight from the strange little dolls.

ZOOM TITLE.

ACT ONE

A series of moving scenes throughout the Club, getting the feel of the place, and the plush—but vulgarly ostentatious, phony status—atmosphere.

Then, Joanna is being mauled by a tipsy patron who tries to proposition her into letting him take her home. She casts about quickly for an alibi, and singles out Tod as he passes nearby, saying, "He's taking me home, aren't you, Tod?" Stiles agrees cheerfully, removing Joanna adroitly from the clutches of the older man. He has been trying to get next to Joanna for weeks, but has concluded that she is more interested in a wealthy suitor. He is pleased by the possible opportunity to see her after work.

Close to closing time that night, one of the security police, Frank Settle, who has also been eyeing Joanna, makes an attempt to take her home, but she withers him with a few words. He makes a small scene, calling her vile names, and Tod hustles the girl from the Club. Settle is a married man, with nine years on the force, whose weak character is goaded by the sight of the indolent rich spending more money in one night than he makes in a month. He hungers for the girls, the glamour, the sense of importance that membership in the Club brings, but he is merely an employee, and only the wearing of the badge daytime keeps him from ruining himself.

Tod gets Joanna into his car, and as they start to her place, she begins to berate herself violently: "Why do I always attracts the wrong ones…? Why can't I ever get a decent man interested in me?" She begins to cry.

Tod has seen the other side of her nature, till now: an amorality that expresses itself in her desire to be near money, in whatever capacity that is possible. But now, in the silence of the 2AM Los Angeles morning, she seems stripped back to that innocence of childhood or nature that speaks more of naïveté than venality.

He suggests they not go home at once, and takes her instead to the Hollywood Ranch Market, an all-night sideshow of Hollywood hangers-on who move colorfully in the background as Tod and Joanna buy breaded hot dogs and root beer, stand and talk. She begins to reveal the story of her trip from England, the time with the Loesser family, her unfortunate affairs. Tod begins to grow toward her, and in swift scenes they drive out to Malibu, walk on the clean sand and hold hands like children, then drive back into the city, to the top of Queens Way Road, where the city spreads out below them like diamond-dust on a black velvet pad.

But as though she is compelled to shatter the mirror-surface of even the smallest peaceful time, Joanna—in the midst of a kiss—breaks away from Tod and stands at the railing over the sheer drop, and shrieks like a harridan at the city, "I'm going to eat you alive! I'm going to stay here, no more dirt, no more crying, never again! I'll do it, you'll see!" and she begins to laugh at the top of her lungs. The eerie silence of this lover's lane is ripped open, and Tod is shocked at her display of emotion.

"Take me out of here, take me home, come home with me, I don't give a damn what happens!"

Tod takes her home, and they make love.

At the same time attracted and repelled by this strange girl, Tod finds himself at ten the next morning, leaving her apartment, and for the first time in many years, at a loss for sense to the situation he has put himself into. It is almost visiting time at the hospital, and he goes to see Buz, telling him he has found a girl who mystifies him, but with whom he may very well swing. Buz is not really amused. There is a shadow on Tod's enthusiasm.

Tod goes in to work later that day, and when he makes a tentative approach to Joanna, she stops him with a harsh, "Get lost, nice guy!"

Tod finds himself in conversation with Settle, who is both arrogant and imploring when it comes to Joanna. In conversation he reveals his frustrations, as Tod and the cop move through the club.

The next morning, Tod receives a call from Joanna. "Let's go on a picnic." They go, Tod drawn almost against his will but compelled to strip away the layers of conflicting personality. They wind up at Griffith Park and what starts out to be a pleasant afternoon is completely ruined when Joanna torments the lions, sending them into a homicidal frenzy. She watches them froth and howl with a delight that is almost animalistic itself.

ACT TWO

Joanna does not come into work. Tod inquires where she is from the *maître d'* and is told she does this every few weeks. She disappears for a night, two nights, then shows up the following evening, and works so hard they cannot bring themselves to let her go.

The next night she appears and Tod asks her where she has been. She stops him sharply by saying just because they spent a night together doesn't mean he has ropes on her. He backs off. A week and a half later, the same thing happens. Again she refuses to explain her whereabouts. On the third occasion, two weeks later, Tod goes looking for her. Settle says he has long been wondering where she goes, and that on his day off he has followed her. He goes with Tod. They find Joanna shacked-up in a sleazy motel up the Coast, with a patron of the Club, the brawny but worthless son of a local business executive.

When the man tries to stop Tod and Settle from taking the drunken and shattered Joanna from the cabin, Settle beats him mercilessly, and is only kept from killing the man by Tod.

Tod persuades Settle to let him take the girl home alone, and when they get to her apartment Tod tries to sober her up. She flares into anger and when he yells at her, "Why? Why the hell are you trying to destroy yourself? You're young and intelligent and good-looking, why are you pouring yourself into the gutter this way?" she replies: "Because I killed my baby, you stupid clown!"

ACT THREE

Tod tries to unravel the twisted skein of Joanna's guilts and learns how her marriage went rotten, how she was left with the child, and in a moment of escape, when she was having an affair with a ne'er-do-well, the baby pulled down an open can of disinfectant, swallowed some and died before she returned from her assignation.

She gets hysterical, and in trying to console her, Tod analyzes her drive to self-destruction as a way of obviating her sins. She constantly throws herself into the path of men who will hurt her, men who will never offer her security, marriage, true love—all the things that led to the death of the child.

"You're not corrupt, Jo," he tells her, "you're like an empty glass, a vessel of some kind, waiting to have the corruption poured into you. Then you go around infecting, like a catalyst, a Typhoid Mary."

She pleads with Tod to help her. He says he isn't sure he can. She throws herself at him, kissing him, hysterically offering herself if he will take care of her, show her how to get straight. She says she has a chance, that he's a good man, and the first who knew, who understood...

Tod agrees, morally blackmailed. But the strain and the constant alterings of her nature are sapping him. The help around the Club remarks that he looks tired, seems nervous.

The next night, Tod sees another patron pawing Jo, and he moves to stop the scene. When he has her away from the man she lashes into him, telling him she can handle her own problems, that the patron was a wealthy oil man and she was flirting with him!

Tod stands helpless before the backsliding of the girl, and later that night is appalled to see her openly carrying on with Settle. He tries to dissuade them both, but Settle gets nasty, and Tod retreats. "Everybody's entitled to go to Hell in his own way," Tod remarks. "And there aren't too many better-looking ways than Joanna."

The days pass and Tod sees Joanna playing Settle like a fish on the line. The man is being destroyed.

Inevitably, enraged, Tod drags her to one side and flings his accusations at her. Joanna's mask is stripped away as she snarls, "If I've got to die, I'll take as many of you with me as I can."

Later that night the owner informs Settle he is through. There is a stringent rule against the girls dating the patrons or the help. The owner tells Settle—in front of Tod—that Joanna has complained that Settle has been annoying her. Settle flips, but is summarily thrown out of the Club.

Jo tries to speak to Tod, in a complete switch of character, tries to explain why she did it, that she is trying to break the chain of unclean events that seem predestined to crush her.

Tod refuses to listen to her story, and they are on the verge of an argument when one of the parking lot boys comes in, white-faced, and tells Tod that Settle got into his car, opened the glove compartment, took out his .38 Police Special and blew half his face off.

ACT FOUR (short act)

After the police have left. Joanna, the vessel and instrument of destruction, has done to Settle what she could not do to Tod. She breaks down, pleads once more for Tod to help her.

Tod's face sets in a determined mask of resolve. He drags her into the car and drives to Settle's home. It is four o'clock in the morning. He rings the bell, and when the door is opened by Settle's widow, Tod tells Joanna viciously, "Explain to her, Jo. Tell *her* how much help you need. Then tell her three kids. Tell them, Jo. Give her the whole tear-jerker. And with luck she'll join your crusade. After this she'll be a ripe candidate."

Then he leaves her, staring at the widow of the man she has murdered.

The next day, Tod hands in his resignation.

As he is leaving, Joanna is going up in the ball. She has been joking with several men as she mounts into the velvet chair, and Tod takes note of her apparent unrepentant attitude by starting to walk away. As the ball slowly rises, Joanna begins to jibe at him:

"Savior! The salvation of American womanhood! You were going to help me, you were going to show me the way!"

Tod paces around in a circle, keeping abreast of her as she goes up into the air on the mirror-faceted ball.

"No one can help you, Jo. Not even yourself, any more. Whoever did this to you did it too well for any Johnny-come-lately like me to undo. It's not you that's the sorry thing, Jo. It's all the people you'll infect before you throw in the sponge.

"There are some people in this life who just shouldn't be allowed to get off the ground, Jo, and you're one of them. Something's got to stop you, before you become a plague. It won't be me, and it may not happen for a long time, but people like you always get put down, Jo.

"It has to happen."

He moves toward the huge front doors of the Club. Joanna's face comes into close-up, drained of bravado, reduced to the ashes of corruption that are her soul. And she sees her last chance walking out the door. "Tod...Tod...come back," she screams, straining at the velvet cord that holds her into the chair. "Come back! I want to know...*I want to know, Tod!*"

But the door has closed, and Tod has gone.

EDITOR'S NOTE: The following were alternate titles listed on the cover page of Ellison's treatment: "A Vessel of Destruction," "The Girl from Far Xanadu," "Pleasure and Pain Mingle in Her," "Eyes of Dust, Soul of Ashes," "The Wrong Girl," "The Girl Who Tormented the Lions," "Shatter the Silence of the Night," "Your Own Personal Devil," "Black, Black Is the Color of My True Love's Soul," "Belladonna, My Love," and "One Lovely Cup of Depravity."

On 3 August 1962, Ellison wrote to a close friend:

…the roof has fallen in here. No work since eight weeks ago; a five-week writer block in which Word #1 would not emerge…a mounting Annapurna of bills unpaid…cut-offs on three tv treatments…the market tightening noose-like…fear…abject cowardice…a horde of twisted girls and kook guys seeking me out like dogs at a fire hydrant (and for the same reason)… unpaid rent…no food…they shut off the water & gas last Monday…

Well, what I'm trying to say is that I *may* be a script writer, but no one is really convinced of that, mostly me, and as long as I'm going to starve, I'd like to starve in a town I like, with people I love, doing work I enjoy, not here in Clown Town, writing garbage for monkeys. There is a strong chance that I will be getting an assignment to write a novel about Hollywood—the editor is flying out from NYC tomorrow, and my agent tells me she wants a book on this village that is "sordid, but sardonic" (her words). If I get the assignment, it will mean an advance of perhaps fifteen hundred or two grand, and on that I can clean up the most pressing bills, and have enough to split town.

The Dick Powell Show—hosted by the eponymous movie star, who periodically appeared in the hour-long plays—was an anthology series produced by Powell's Four Star Production for NBC. The showcase ran for two seasons from 26 September 1961 to 17 September 1963, the title changing to *The Dick Powell Theatre* after the host's death from lung cancer on 3 January 1963.

As with *Route 66*, Ellison drew on his stint at *Rogue*, which becomes *Debonair* magazine. "All That Glitters" borrows a lot of its author's recent past to inform the protagonist, Harry Ashton. It was likely written and submitted in late 1962—before the show's title changed to reflect Powell's death, though it *could* have been written as late as April 1963, by which time *Powell's* producers Aaron Spelling and Richard Newton were preparing to launch *Burke's Law* for the 1963–4 season.

By 25 April 1963, *Debonair* magazine was the setting for "Even Demon's Die," a storyline that would evolve—over the next three months—into Ellison's first episode of *Burke's Law*, "Who Killed Alex Debbs?" and lead to a burgeoning screenwriting career. [Ellison's four credited contributions to Burke's Law appear in BRAIN MOVIES, Volumes 3–6.]

All That Glitters

The Dick Powell Show (ca. 1962–1963)

It looks like a golden life: plenty of good-looking girls, fast cars, swinging night life, and prestige. It looks like *the* good life, as Harry Ashton arrives in Chicago to work on *Debonair Magazine*. At any rate, it's a better scene than the one from which he has recently emerged.

With his marriage messily ended, two years in a dreary Southern Army post behind him, and his wallet empty, a chance to do some plain and fancy editing on the top girlie magazine in the country—close to two million monthly circulation—is the next thing to Paradise. And for a writer like Harry, whose novelistic career has been kept in suspended animation for two years of military service, it is a chance to regain a semblance of living, a chance to find himself again.

But working for *Debonair* involves more than just sitting behind a typewriter, hacking out copy. It means playing office politics with Raymond Jason's staff, and his second-in-command, hatchetman Ernie Norvo. For Jason has built himself a publishing empire on the face and form of lovely women, and half the job is keeping up the attitude that the *Debonair* life is the *only* life. Yet Harry begins to suffer twinges of doubt as the days of partying, wenching, and drinking merge into a glittery ball of wasted hours and shallow relationships.

Jason is impressed with Harry and his background, and takes him into his confidence. Despite the heavy sugar *Debonair* brings in, it is only a bagatelle compared to the undercover, non-taxable income Jason and Norvo collect recruiting girls through the magazine for stag films, bachelor parties, and other traffics in female flesh.

Harry is appalled, but holds back comment when he sees the cunning Norvo taking his measure.

And so the weeks progress, with Harry attending the parties, doing his office work, and getting further and further embroiled in the materialistic, but empty, *Debonair* routine.

At one of the parties thrown in Jason's vulgarly ostentatious town house, Harry meets a girl who has posed for the magazine, now employed at the *Debonair* Key Club, where many ex-*Debonair* girls fill out their contracts with Jason. Her name is Monica Holloway, and her view of Jason, his empire, and the life they are all living so tallies with Harry's, that they become friends, and a romance ensues.

Despite Harry's growing disillusionment with Jason and his hypocritical attitude that *Debonair* is a magazine setting tastes and trends for the young American male, his relationship with Monica pleasures him enough so that he is able to rationalize his existence, and not grow surly or depressed.

Then, comes the kicker. Jason calls in Monica, tells her there are too many girls coming up in the job-sequence for the Key Club, and that he will have to shift her to another job in the organization, to fill out the term of her contract. He bluntly informs her she will become an "escort" for wealthy visitors to the city, and for men who can do the magazine some good. She refuses, knowing very well what Jason means under his oily explanation of her duties.

Ernie Norvo steps in and lays it right on the line. "A bottle of acid would fix your chances of ever modeling again. I think you'd better take Mr. Jason's offer." She accedes to their wishes, and tells Harry later that he must not do anything to interfere, or they will both wind up on the street, much the worse for wear.

Harry realizes now just how corrupt Jason and his system have become. He wants to do something, but the years in poverty, the flashy life he has become accustomed to, all combine to smother his strength, and he agrees to let her work out her situation by herself.

The following week, Monica is sent on her first "escort" job by Jason.

The publisher warns her, however, to be very careful who she talks to, for there are rumors of a Senate investigation of obscenity as allied to the call girl and pornography industries. He tells her their public image on *Debonair* has successfully kept the snoopers away till now, but any wrong moves on anyone's part could sink the boat.

She goes to her "escort" job, an orgy-like party of advertising executives being plied with goodies by *Debonair* in hopes of getting more ad space commitments.

The party grows wilder, and in an attempt to escape a drunken lecher, Monica is thrown against a window, and plunges from the hotel room to the street below.

Harry is called to the morgue to identify the girl, and in the presence of what he has allowed to happen by his weakness, he swears to make her death a costly one for Jason, Norvo, and the entire foul machinery of the *Debonair* scene.

He goes to Jason's home, and there confronts him with not only his resignation, but the promise that within the week he will blow the whistle on all the sub-cutaneous activities of the organization. "I'm going to howl long and loud, Jason," he says, "and your little house of pink cards is going to come down right on your head."

Jason panics and tries to brace Harry with Norvo. A fight ensues, and Harry barely manages to escape from the house.

He knows he may never again sell a novel or work on a magazine, for Jason will surely have him blackballed; may even have him killed. But he is going to tell it all, going to reveal the sterile, arid life that *Debonair* is selling to two million impressionable and frustrated American males. And he is going to reveal the dirt and quicksand foundation on which *Debonair* rests, the wholesale use of women for Jason's profit.

He may have sold out his future for a principle, but what other choice has he, when a corpse on a slab in the morgue cries out in horror at his weakness?

Harry Ashton has begun to find his way home.

At some point—probably 1962—Ellison adapted his own novella "Run for the Stars" for American-International Pictures. In AMERICAN INTERNATIONAL PICTURES: *The Golden Years* (Bear Manor Media, 2013), author Gary A. Smith referenced Ellison scripting a $2 million epic titled *War of the Planets* to star Vincent Price and Boris Karloff, but whether that relates to this treatment—naming Jack Palance—is a question for the custodian of AIP's archives. What *is* known is that Ellison's break on *Burke's Law did* lead to work with AIP, as he wrote to his friend on 18 December 1963:

> Since you left, the most incredible things have happened to me, it literally staggers the mind in retelling. ... I was unable to write at all, a single word, a thought, a story, a script, anything, for seventeen of the most hellish weeks in my life. ... I broke through the bonds of my own psychoses and the machinery of the System here in Hollywood, and started scripting like a madman. I wound up making forty thousand dollars this year, with eight shows on "Burke's Law", the sale of "Rumble" for ten grand to American-International Pictures ... When it broke, it really broke.

"The Darkness Behind Their Eyes" was probably developed during the 1962–3 season, prior to Ellison's stint on *Burke's Law*. He dictated the premise on an extant reel of audiotape, and the story is very much of a piece with the socially conscious, mainstream prose work that dominated Ellison's output in the early Sixties.

Hot off scripting *The Oscar* in 1965, Ellison returned to Four Star Television. The success of *The Man from U.N.C.L.E.* had inspired the powers-that-be to reformat *Burke's Law*, making the titular homicide captain into the aptly—but prosaically—titled *Amos Burke, Secret Agent*. At the same time, Four Star was launching a spinoff based on the Honey West books by G. G. Fickling, starring Ann Francis, who'd guest starred in a two-part *Burke's Law* the previous season.

Ellison took a crack at both shows, submitting "Mrs. Pigsfoot" to *Honey West* on 19 May 1965 and "In the Valley of the Winds" to *Amos Burke, Secret Agent* less than a week later on 25 May. Neither treatment advanced to teleplay, though Ellison took another crack at *Honey West* later in the year, landing a script assignment on "Honey Goes Ape!" *Honey West* and *Amos Burke, Secret Agent* were both cancelled, and Ellison moved on to *U.N.C.L.E.* [See BRAIN MOVIES, Vols. 6 & 2 for *West* and *U.N.C.L.E.*]

Ellison later learned that his usage of the word gunsel in the *Honey West* script was incorrect—see "A Gunsel Is Not a Pistolero."

Run for the Stars
(ca. 1962–1963)

FADE IN:

The screen is black. Total, empty black. In the upper left of the black frame is a medium-sized white dot. Softly, insistently, we hear the beat of music behind. Then, from the lower right of the frame comes the tiny figure of a man—dead-white against the stark black of the frame— running; frantic, terrified, fitful starts and stops as though trapped, seeking some exit. The figure rushes across the lower third of the frame, then plunges off screen left as the first title is snapped on the black background:

RUN FOR THE STARS

The figure appears again, rushing onto the screen from left-center as the title vanishes. He flings himself directly across the screen and off right as the second title snaps on screen:

STARRING JACK PALANCE

The figure appears again as the second title snaps off; center right, rushes halfway across screen, stumbles, falls, picks himself up looks back over shoulder, while the great white dot hangs motionless above him. Then he plunges off screen left as SUBSEQUENT TITLES ARE FLASHED.

This pattern continues till all titles have been flashed and the music has built to a crescendo. As the title

PRODUCED BY JAMES H. NICHOLSON

vanishes from the screen, the tiny white man appears at the center rear of the screen, and rushes headlong toward us, growing larger and larger as though he will charge directly into the camera. When he has reached the middle foreground he careens to an abrupt stop, spins, and looks up over his shoulder at the white dot. Like a sun going nova, the white dot *explodes*!

Terrified, the man plunges forward again, rushes headlong at us as the frame flashes blindingly, glaringly white...

CAMERA MOVES IN ON the white, trucking forward as though through some dense white substance, and as it moves in deeper and deeper, we see the white getting murky, faintly gray, then dirtier gray and even more, almost like fog, or smoke, thick smoke...and suddenly we realize it is smoke, and we moving down through it. Patches begin to tear away in the smoke blanket as the CAMERA CONTINUES DOWN as through clouds of the thick, oily substance. Through the patches we see shapes beginning to take form, and then, suddenly, we finally burst through to see it is the smoke rising from a bombed and decimated city.

We have made the transition from titles to story-proper.

CAMERA DESCENDS on city. At first we have a wide angle view from above of almost total destruction. As though a giant hand had smashed flat everything daring to reach toward the sky. Craters and the charred, smoking stumps of buildings. Carnage and the twisted carcasses of vehicles run up over sidewalks, through store windows; lamp posts twisted like copper coil; bodies sprawled in the streets, still lying where they were struck down. Throughout the decent through the smoke and the decent over the city, NARRATION OVER:

"This is a tomorrow. Perhaps not *the* tomorrow that awaits us, but a possibility. A tomorrow in which Mother Earth had sent out its children to the stars. Fighting, seeking, loving—as all its children had been, since first they learned to walk erect. A tomorrow on another world, not circling this sun or the sun that is the nearest star we see in the night sky. A sun millions of light years buried in the dust-heaps that comprise the universe. And on that planet, circling that sun, in that tomorrow, not necessarily *your* tomorrow, Earth's children met their greatest challenge—and found their only salvation lay in the most worthless man among them."

As NARRATION CONTINUES OVER we GO WITH CAMERA as it descends further; as CAMERA ANGLE TIGHTENS, we see movement in and among the buildings...a group of people, carrying odd weapons, some sort of futuristic rifles perhaps, clumped together, a scouting party of guerrillas...they slip from alley to doorway, from street to storefront, keeping close to the blasted walls. The CAMERA GOES WITH them FROM ABOVE still high enough over the streets to give a labyrinth impression of the men moving through cross-alleys and passages almost like mice in a maze.

CAMERA DESCENDS further, coming down to waist-level in an intersection, so we still see the advancing group of men, but also have a direct view of several shattered storefronts. CAMERA MOVES IN on one of these stores, going till it enters through the broken plate glass of the front window, and we see that the dim movement we have sensed as the camera moved in, is actually a man, bent over a corpse, busily working at it. CAMERA HOLDS on him as he frantically loots the body, then:

REVERSE ANGLE as we see it is Benno Tallant, face filthy with soot and dirt, a pistol strapped across his chest, the holster just below his left armpit. Tallant is intent upon what he is doing, but it is as if his face was focused upon us, so distant, so singular it is. There is cruelty in the chiseled planes and shadowed cavities, and a touch of despair, and something else—perhaps fear.

The dead shopkeeper is wearing a bib-like affair with many pockets, and Tallant is systematically, but hurriedly, going through each one. As CAMERA HOLDS, we see through the shattered storefront behind Tallant, the advancing party of guerrillas, coming across the intersection, slipping from cover to cover. They are held up by their leader who points across the street, through the window, at Tallant. The looter knows nothing of this as he works at his ghoulish chore.

CAMERA HOLDS as the group slips across the street, and into the store behind Benno Tallant. They walk carefully, catlike, to avoid the noise of debris underfoot. We are close in on Tallant as he works over the shopkeeper and CAMERA HAS MOVED IN TIGHT so we get a head and shoulders shot of him, studying the hard, cruel face. Then, suddenly, an arm goes around his neck, he is jerked up out of the frame so we are sighting at his belt buckle. He struggles, slips sidewise revealing the scene behind him, and we see a woman advancing behind him, the butt of her rifle ready to strike. We hear a sharp crack as the blow is landed, and Tallant slumps. CAMERA PULLS IN TIGHT as the body—still at belt buckle level—is dragged out of the frame, and we see his boot-heels making two furrows in the plaster dust of the floor. CAMERA HOLDS on the twin tracks, and the limp hand of the dead shopkeeper lying in the F. G.

CAMERA CLOSES on hand as we dissolve THRU IDENTICAL SHOT to another hand, lying in the same position...limp at the side of a man. A leather strap holds the hand in place. CAMERA PULLS UP & BACK and we realize we are *again* looking down on a scene. As CAMERA RISES we see we are in some sort of hastily jerry-rigged operating room, and the white walls angle down to fill most of the frame, leaving only the center—the bottom of a square well, as it were—for the sharp action transpiring there. And in the center of that well, Benno Tallant is strapped to a table as a surgeon and two aides work over him. We see the military men who captured him lounging against the walls, and the woman who struck him, watching interestedly from a corner. The surgeons keep busy over Tallant's body, but we cannot see what they are doing.

One of the aides goes to a cabinet, takes out a square black box, and brings it to the operating table. The surgeon steps back, and we see that the sheet covering Benno Tallant has a hole cut out of it. The sheet has been sewed down, pegged down, around his body, and his stomach has been laid open. CAMERA ZOOMS IN to CU of Tallant's face, as he comes out from under the anesthetic. He raises his head, looks down his body at the activity going on, and CAMERA HOLDS on expression of stark horror. QUICK CUT TO REVERSE ANGLE of WHAT HE SEES:

They are operating on him. His stomach has been laid open. They are beginning to insert the small black, knobbed and calibrated box into his stomach. His body strains against the straps holding him. The surgeon's face comes up and he stares back at Tallant as we QUICK CUT to PREVIOUS SHOT of Tallant's face. Eyes widening in horror, he is on the verge of screaming as a hand darts in from off screen, pressing a wad of cotton against his mouth and nose. It is obviously an anesthetic, and as he struggles, his eyes roll up and he slumps back, asleep again.

The operation proceeds, and as it goes on, as we hear the surgeon's voice—hollowly, as though reverberating down an echoing corridor—Benno Tallant's comatose dreams are flashed before our eyes...even as he sees them behind *his* eyes:

We see his planet, this world on which he sleeps; we see Earth; and we see a third world. A world inhabited by golden-skinned creatures very much like humans, save their hands end in silken tentacles rather than fingers, their eyes are wide, round, and lidless, and they are the color of molten gold: the Kyben.

Almost in pictograph fashion we see the Kyben send out their spaceships, begin to explore the universe. We see Earth sending her own ships to the stars, men settling other worlds, *this* world. And we see the first clash in space of the Human-Kyben fleets; a fierce electric battle raging across the deeps of space, and both retreating. As one vision chases another, we see the Kyben fleet pulling back, then massing for an attack. We see scout ships of the main fleet streak off toward this world where Benno Tallant sleeps. We see the other scouts turn away, for other worlds, and one gigantic spaceship hover over this world. We see it send out smaller attack vessels, and in a few moments of dreamtime, we see those attack vessels level the cities. We see an Earthship try to take off, to warn the mother planet, and we see it vaporized by the alien vessel hanging overhead. As Benno Tallant's dream-coma continues he sees the land forces destroyed, the scoutships from the huge Kyben vessel strafing and burning the cities, individual scenes of slaughter in the streets. He sees the Resistance wiped away, leaving only a handful, among them the ones who brought him to this operating room. He sees the scene of his capture...sees the operation...sees them inserting that somehow terrifying black cube in his stomach...and as he reaches that point in his visions, he slips back to consciousness. *(End special effects shots & surgeon's voice under.)*

SCENE swims into FOCUS as Benno Tallant awakes from anesthetic. ELONGATED SHOT as Tallant stares up into the white tunnel of the walls meeting ceiling. (*REVERSE SHOT of previous downlooking angle of Tallant on operating table.*) Heads appear in his line of vision. He sees the leader of the guerrillas who captured him—strong and determined face; weathered from too much responsibility, too much fighting, too little sleep; split by a raw scar that burns in one cheek—and he sees the stubble-bearded face of the surgeon who worked on him, eyes rheumy, nose crimson, all the signposts of a drunkard. And he sees the girl. The young, lovely features overlayed with a film of dirt and soot-smudges... and something else. Viciousness, a barely-restrained violence that erases all her youth, giving her the appearance of a beautiful, deadly beast of the fields. It is her face that registers most profoundly with Benno as his gaze is held by hers.

At first their faces appear indistinct as Benno returns from his coma, but as we hear their voices coming remotely, then stronger, echoing, down that long corridor, they COME INTO FOCUS.

"How do you feel?" the Resistance leader asked.

There is no warmth in his voice, no real concern, only the tone of a man with a job to do, wanting to know if the proper tools are ready.

Tallant is seen in reverse angle, wetting his lips. He seems somehow wasted away, dried out, as though just having come in off a desert. He moves his hand slightly and seems ready to ask for some water, but instead says:

TALLANT
(eyes squeezed shut in pain)
I—I hurt. I n-need a fix...give me a...fix.
(presses stomach in pain)

GIRL
(turns viciously to others)
A junkie! A dust-dreamer! You picked a lousy
dustie!

Leader waves her impatiently to silence. Turns to surgeon.

LEADER

Doc? Will this get in the way of what we need
done?

DOC
(scratches chin, shrugs)
Hell, don't see why it should. Might even make
it better. Withdrawal, it'll keep him runnin' for
a fix.
(beat)
That's what you're lookin' for, isn't it...to keep
him on the move?
(Leader nods. Doc shrugs)
Well, then that only makes it harder for him to
stand still.

GIRL
(interrupting)
No good! I don't trust a junkie!

LEADER

Shut up!

Tallant has been listening to all this. Now, suddenly, he gets violent.

TALLANT
What do you want with me...what are you
trying to do to me...
(Beat, as he remembers the black
box in his stomach)
What was that you put inside me? What was it...
tell me...what have you done...

His hysteria builds, higher and higher, and they grab him, force him to
lie down.

LEADER
Doc! Put him under again! Quick!

> DOC
> (grabs ærosol-spray syringe)
> Hold him, he'll open those incisions!

Doc tries to get at Tallant's writhing body as the others hold him down, finally pushes through, aims the syringe and sprays the anesthetic into Tallant's chest. Tallant slumps almost at once, gives a final spastic twitch, then lies silently.

> GIRL
> (viciously)
> A junkie! Beautiful! One whiff of the dust and he's hooked for life...he'd sellout his children to an axe-murderer for a fix!

> LEADER
> Listen, just put a bag over it, will you! I've got enough on my mind without you raising the noise level.
> (turns to Doc, worriedly)
> What about that stomach? Think he did any damage?

> DOC
> (examining livid scar on Tallant's abdomen)
> No, I don't think so. I'll put the Rejuvenator on him.

Goes to bank of machines, wheels out a portable instrument on a stand, unhooks long, segmented metal hose, arranges it so its bell-shaped mouth is focused down on Tallant's stomach from above. He turns to Leader.

> DOC
> This'll seal and replace the damaged tissue.

Clicks the machine on. A thin blue beam washes Tallant's abdomen, and as we watch, the angry crimson scar begins to pucker and heal over where the incisions had been.

> DOC
> He'll be ready for you in about three hours.
> Have you got that long?

> LEADER
> (ruefully)
> If we haven't, we'll all be dead in three hours...
> and he'll be the luckiest one of all...he won't
> know when it happens.

They leave him.

CAMERA DOLLIES IN on Tallant lying drugged under the healing blue ray, and the room is SILENT, though faintly, as though from far off, we hear the SOUND OF BOMBING.

We hear the sound of DOOR OPENING O.S. and CAMERA PANS SMOOTHLY to door as the girl enters. CAMERA GOES WITH HER as she walks to Tallant, stares down at him, a look of hatred coming over her face. She stares at him for a long moment then moves OFF-CAMERA as we HOLD on Tallant. From O.S. we hear the door open and close again, as we

> FADE OUT.

FADE IN with screen black, suddenly yanked forward as we see the blackness has been Tallant's body lying on the operating table. He is yanked erect by a huge, bull-necked man named Shep, one of the original group who captured him. Shep throws him a bundle of clothes, tells him to get dressed, that Parkhurst wants to see him. Tallant cannot manage the dressing himself, and Shep is forced to do it, almost as though Benno were an infant. In the process, Tallant is shaking so badly from dust-withdrawal, that he tries to get Shep to steal him a fix. Shep slaps him, drags him off the table and herds him down a sandbag-reinforced corridor. It is obvious they are underground, and as they move through the dim passages of the Resistance headquarters, the sound of bombs and strafing come dimly from far away. Suddenly, a soft whistling is heard, Shep bodily lifts Tallant, and dives blindly down the tunnel. Behind them, where they stood, a deafening explosion rips the air and the tunnel is half caved in as tons of dirt and rock and red-hot metal come blasting down.

Shep hurries Tallant on, and they finally enter the communications center. Banks of transmitters cover the walls, lights phasing and scurrying across the dials and capacitors. The leader, the one Shep called Parkhurst, stands talking to the Doc and the girl and another man. They stop talking as Tallant enters.

Parkhurst introduces the surgeon as Doc Budder, the girl as Willie and the other man as Vice-President Dixon, a foppish, cowardly politician, last of the governing body of this planet and the only member of that body to escape death when the government centers were destroyed. The feeling is clear that Dixon's escape was not mere chance. He spends his time decrying the "traitors that bored from within" and continually tries to convince Parkhurst they should throw themselves on the mercy of the Kyben. The leader of the resistance, however, ignores Dixon.

Tallant demands to know what he is doing here, why they have operated on him, and what it was that was grafted into his stomach. Parkhurst is about to tell him, when a technician at the controls signals. Parkhurst waves Tallant to silence, and takes a hand-mike from the technician. A screen on the communications panel begins to glow, a wash of pastel colors runs milkily across its surface, and suddenly it solidifies to show the Kyben flagship, a mile-high structure rising out of the bombed rubble of the city. Parkhurst speaks into the mike:

PARKHURST
This is the leader of the human colony. I
want to speak to your Commander. I'll give
you fifteen minutes to put your translating
machines on this message. This is of immediate
importance to you. Fifteen minutes to get
your Commander or I destroy this planet and
everyone on it.

Almost immediately, the picture melts, runs like watercolors and solidifies to the image of a golden Kyben officer, uniform resplendent with braid. They are so human, these Kyben, yet so alien, that their appearance is far more imposing, far more terrifying than if they had been totally divorced from mankind in shape. The differences—the hands ending in silken, wavering tentacles; the lidless, staring eyes; flat, large-nostrilled noses; the deep yellow ochre color of their hairless bodies—are so noticeable, that the sight of them is like seeing a graveyard-full of decaying corpses walking.

The Commander comes onscreen, and from the speaker grille in the panel comes a burst of static, then a frenzied rush of alien speech. Parkhurst snaps his fingers at the technician: "The translator, quick!"

The sibilant, hissing sound of the Kyben speech is cut off in the middle of a sound as the translator cuts in, and the hissing is turned into human speech. On the screen—like a dubbed movie—the alien still hisses his Kyben tongue, but from the grille pours the furious demands of an alien race. Parkhurst cuts him off, and tells the Commander:

PARKHURST
(matter-of-factly)
We have planted a sun-bomb, on the planet.
I don't know if your science is capable of
producing a weapon of this kind, so I will show
you its power. Watch your screens.

He motions to his technicians. The face of the Kyben commander vanishes, the picture swirls until the technician threads a film into the viewer, and then as he cuts it in, the picture wavers, swims, and solidifies once more to show a solar system of fifteen planets. The scene in the viewer moves in on the tenth planet of that system, cuts to a team laying a sun-bomb. Scene shifts to a spaceship hanging outside the orbit of the farthest planet from the sun and goes inside show a technician triggering the bomb. The scene cuts back to a medium close-up of the planet with the bomb, and we hear a countdown from ten to one. Then the planet explodes. A hellfire of red then yellow then white-hot flames and gasses leaps up as the camera moves back. The two nearest planets catch, then two more. The camera draws back rapidly until it is outside the solar system once more, and we see planets by one and two and three exploding, until the very sun of that system goes nova, filling the entire screen with a blinding, blazing torment of fury and destruction. Then, abruptly as if the film had been destroyed, the screen goes black. Parkhurst motions for the technician to cut him back in to the Kyben commander. There is fear on the alien face of the golden man when it returns to the screen.

PARKHURST

The ship that took those films was destroyed.
Only parts of it were found floating in the area
of the asteroid belt formed by the destruction
of that system. We have never put this bomb
to use in battle for its power is so great that
it destroys not only those against whom it is
employed, but those who trigger it. One of
those bombs is set and triggered, now, here,
on this planet. Don't try to take off, for if you
do, we will set it off at once. We have nothing
to lose. Our only hope is to convince you that
what I say is true, and bargain with you for
our freedom. If you let us take off, every man,
woman, and child left alive on this world, we
will promise not to detonate the bomb, to leave
you here with the opportunity of finding and
deactivating it before it goes off. It is our only
offer. You have one hour to decide.

The realization dawns with horror. Tallant knows now what the small black box in his stomach must be. Inside him...a sun-bomb. Enough power to blow this entire solar system to ashes. Terror grips him. He tries to flee the blockhouse. They grab him and hold him down. He becomes hysterical, complains of terrible pains in his stomach. Doc Budder snorts, "Self-induced cramp." Tallant cries that he needs a fix of narcotics. He tries to break away. Parkhurst and Shep stop him.

Parkhurst tries to explain: "Listen to me, fella. If it hadn't been you, it would have been someone else. We needed someone to keep running after we're gone. They'll have radiation emission detectors, and if we planted that bomb underground or in a stationary object, they'd home in on it in ten minutes, and vaporize our ships before we'd left this system. We've got to have time. To warn Earth. If we don't, they'll move on from here and nothing can stop them."

Tallant blurts, "Why don't you use *those* to call Earth." He motions toward the sub-space transmitters.

Parkhurst shakes his head. "Too far. Solar interference. We haven't got the juice. We have to get back to Earth, or at least an outpost close enough to send out a message."

"Why me? Why not Shep or Doc Budder...or *her*! Or *anybody*? But why me?"

The girl snaps a vicious answer, "Because you're scum. Who'll miss you? You lousy dustie! A looter, a bum, not worth the powder to blow you to hell! That's why! We aren't going to waste a decent human being when we've got a rotten little coward like you..."

Tallant is being sentenced to death. No matter what decision is made by the Kyben, he will die. The bomb has already been set, it will go off automatically.

"We control it now," Parkhurst tells him, "but when we leave this solar system, we throw it into automatic. Then, the Kyben have to find it before it goes off."

Tallant's eyes widen in horror. "But...but...you told them it can be damped, disconnected, turned off! You were lying...there's no way to stop it!"

"Maybe," Parkhurst replies, looking away.

"You'll keep running if you don't know, for sure, dustie," the girl, Willie, snarls.

"Stop calling me dustie! I've got a name!" Tallant screams.

Parkhurst interrupts quickly, "Don't tell me, fella. I don't want to know your name."

"Why? Too rough on you to know the name of the man you're killing? Is that it? You rotten bunch of *patriots*! Is that it, you don't want me to have a name, or a life, just leave me here to die, while you all run away? Is that it?"

The communicator bleeps, and the Kyben commander comes back on. "You have permission to leave. Our detectors have taken an emission count, and we believe you. We have no choice. You may take off."

The humans begin preparations for takeoff.

Tallant tries to intimidate them. "I won't run. I'll let them find me, I'll let them take out the bomb! I don't owe you anything!"

Willie laughs evilly. "You won't do that."

"Why?"

"Because the Kyben won't be as gentle as Doc Budder was. They'll think we're all gone. If they catch you, all they'll do is blast you down and ask questions after. Except there won't be any questions, because that bomb is triggered to go off in case you get killed. It's hooked into your nervous system. Or if you *do* get through to them, they'll cut it out...the hard way."

They leave Tallant in the blockhouse, and begin loading the ships. The remaining humans on the planet are hurried aboard the few ships intact. Tallant goes with them to the spaceport, pleading piteously to be taken with them. As Parkhurst goes aboard he says, "It doesn't count for much, but I'm sorry. Real sorry we have to do this. But it means the lives of everyone on Earth and all the planets from here to there."

He enters the ship, the port seals itself, and the sub-space generators begin to hum. Tallant flees back to the blockhouse, watches as the ships take off.

Suddenly his terror and his weak nature combine to produce a withdrawal fit only the dream-dust can end. He goes berserk, wrecks the blockhouse in search of dust, and finally comes across Doc Budder's office. There he finds a cache of medicinal dust, used for calming hysteria. He takes a solid whiff and begins to compose himself.

He decides to get away from the spaceport and the blockhouse before the Kyben come in search. *This is the first place they'll look for that bomb*, he thinks.

But the dust is taking effect. He leans against the wall, steadying himself.

Suddenly, the door bursts open and a Kyben trooper, with blast-rifle poised, stands there. But Tallant has been behind the door, leaning against the wall. He sees the alien before the alien sees him. He grabs for the rifle, pulls it from the hands of the trooper, and swings it viciously, crushing the alien's golden head.

He is about to bolt from the blockhouse when he looks at one of the still-working telescreens. The spacefield is swarming with Kyben troopers, some riding one-man flitters, the others running across the landing strip.

He drags the body of the Kyben trooper to the trapdoor leading to the underground headquarters, throws the body down, and leaps after it. He pulls the trap shut and sits quaking in fear as the aliens storm the blockhouse.

They clump about overhead while he sits with blaster ready, but they do not discover the trapdoor, and finally leave. He knows the spaceport will be overrun with Kyben, so he decides to seek an exit at the other end of the passages.

After digging through the caved-in sections, he finds an escape exit in the woods at the perimeter of the spaceport, and flees into them, realizing bitterly that he is doing precisely what the humans wanted him to do—he is running, gaining time for them. And he vows vengeance, somehow, some way.

Tallant wanders across the primitive frontier planet, evading the Kyben patrols. He gets as far as the Blue Marshes, a vast dark swamp, before he collapses, exhausted. The dust is wearing off, and he opens a fresh packet, ready to sniff, when he hears a snort, a sound of something living, nearby. He pauses, the packet almost to his face, as the sound of something huge, heavy, moving through the swamp comes nearer, nearer. He is paralyzed with fear, sitting on the upthrust root of a great, strange tree. As he sits immobile, the sound grows to incredible loudness, and he turns slowly...

To face a gigantic creature from a nightmare. Big as a house, it rises. Deep blue-black, with eyes like the many-faceted honeycomb of a bee's-eye. Vaguely similar to a brontosaurus, its differences spell the meat-eater, rather than the vegetarian:

Gigantic, swollen body. Eight legs, four to a side, set under the body so the creature hangs over on all sides. Smooth, oily hide with a cluster of twitching cilia halfway up the chest. A long, thick snakelike neck rising high and curving into the air, ending in a triangular head. A wide gash of a mouth framed by more twitching silken fibers, a pair of vise-grip jaws, and double rows of spike teeth above and below. A long, forked tongue, hinged from the front, whips in and out, in and out. And those eyes. Those two terrible diamond-faceted flaming orbs of crimson.

TWO-SHOT of Tallant staring at beast. CAMERA DOLLIES IN slowly, slowly on the two red eyes, showing us WHAT HE SEES. Then, abruptly, INTERCUT to PROCESS SHOT in red of the scene before the beast, Tallant, shown in a hundred facets, as though we were staring out of the creature's eyes. FRAME HOLDS in many-prismed shot, and we see Tallant in stark terror, a hundred times over.

Then REVERSE ANGLE in NORMAL SHOT of Tallant again. He bolts, trips, sprawls over the root, and the blast rifle is flung into the swamp, sucked under instantly.

The creature lumbers forward. Tallant screams, falls back, unable to move in the thick muck of the swamp. Creature rises up trumpeting terrifyingly, head lashed back to strike, to tear Tallant apart.

Suddenly, a wash of blue blast-flame leaps out of the swamp, bathing the maddened creature. The beast rises as high as it can go, straining its ghastly neck, whipping it about, turning its head, its insane eyes flickering. It tries to turn, to flee, but the blast-flame licks at it, holds it, a coruscating aurora of deadly light, and then—the creature explodes, dead carcass tumbling into the swamp. As Tallant regains his senses from the concussion, he sees the beast's corpse twitching in final reflex spasm, and then, slowly, moistly, the carcass is sucked down and down and disappears from sight in the quagmire. It is gone, and except for the million sounds of the swamp, there is silence once more.

Tallant crouches behind the root, waiting to see what new danger is responsible for his being saved from the creature. He hears sucking footsteps as whoever fired the blast comes toward him. He snaps off a length of root and wields it, ready to smash in the face of whoever it can be—for on this dead world the only other thinking creatures, the only other ones with blasters—the Kyben.

The footsteps near, and from around the thick bole of the swamp-tree—the girl, Willie.

The last man on this world is no longer alone.

She had not trusted Parkhurst's plan. If there was even a chance that Tallant would defect to the Kyben and take his chances, she was going to see that chance eliminated. She had slipped off her ship, had started back for the blockhouse, but had been forced to hide when the Kyben troops invaded the field. Seeing them ransacking the blockhouse, and not finding Tallant, she knew he must have found the escape exit, and had struck out for it. She had been trailing him since he had entered the Blue Marshes. Her open hatred for him causes Tallant to take a long second look at the girl. Later that night, having captured a swamp creature, eating it raw (a fire might draw Kyben attention), Tallant tries to get at the basis of her attitude.

The girl finally tells him of her father who had been a junkie, a dust-dreamer who had driven her mother to suicide. She swears hatred for all junkies, they're loathsome, untrustworthy, cowards. Yet there is something different about Benno Tallant. He is something more than the craven looter who was captured by Parkhurst. Is it the dust he has been swilling? Or the inevitability of the death lodged in his gut? Or the Kyben slowly and certainly tracking him to his doom? Or something else?

During the night they see lights from flitters hovering just above the ground, searching the Blue Marshes. They strike out again, with no destination in mind save to keep ahead of the Kyben patrols until they are homed-in on, by the heat sensors, and hope that the ships have gotten far enough away so pursuit by the Kyben is impossible.

That is the girl's hope.

It is not Benno Tallant's hope.

A series of encounters with Kyben patrols. The first, in the Glass Mountains—towering, opaque crystal formations—results in a Kyben trooper getting off a message to the flagship that there are humans alive on the planet. The second, in which Tallant is wounded, burned across the chest, saving Willie's life, brings them, oddly, not closer together, but more determined in their hatred for one another. Tallant realizes that it is only a matter of time until the Kyben, getting different readings on the emission from the sun-bomb, will figure out that it is not stationary, that it is in a moving object; that, coupled with the trooper's dying message, will tell them their target is the last man alive on this planet.

He decides his only chance is to get to the Kyben before they get to him. If he is discovered by common foot-soldiers, they will shoot first, and explode the bomb. But if he can get to the Commander on the flagship, then there is a chance for a proper deactivation, a proper operation, and a chance to offer his services to the Kyben in their war against Earth.

After all, what does he owe the humans who left him to die, with a bomb in his belly?

But he cannot tell the girl that.

He convinces her the only chance they have is to get to the flagship and do what damage they can, in the event he is captured and the bomb deactivated. She looks at him with fresh eyes...has the coward, the dustie, the looter, changed his tune? Has he started on the path to being a decent human being? Is that courage he's displaying?

They strike out for the alien flagship.

They capture a flitter. Back to the city. They hole up temporarily in the bombed-out shell of what had been the water-works. Willie tells him this leads to the sewers, that they can follow the pipes to an outlet near the ship itself. That night a Kyben patrol almost discovers them, but Tallant kills the aliens by stealth and by hand. The change in him is more apparent now; he has picked up much of the cruel viciousness of the Marsh creatures, and the responsibility of staying alive has hardened him. Willie realizes he has not had a whiff of dust for almost two days. Tallant does not reveal the source of his newfound strength: hatred of the men who left him to die; a silent oath to see them in hell.

They leave the building next morning, down into the sewers. A fight with the giant rats who live there. Yellow eyes glowing, the hordes of starving rodents almost drag them down. They manage to escape, find an outlet near the Kyben ship. Tallant kills a guard, and they enter the ship. Instead of stairwells or escalators, the mile-high flagship has suction-tubes, droplifts; they whisk passengers from floor to floor.

The ship is nearly deserted. All available aliens are out seeking the man with the bomb in his stomach. They see an alien in a white tunic walking through a corridor. A doctor.

They capture him, and Tallant uses his dream-dust to make the Doctor an addict. One whiff and the alien is a willing slave of the drug. Tallant demands he operate, take out the sun-bomb. A combination of addiction, gunpoint and fear convince the Doctor. Tallant says he'll have the operation without anesthetic. The Doctor performs the operation. It is long and painful, but Tallant stays awake and alert all through it, the blaster pointed at the alien. The operation is a success. The bomb is removed and damped. But Tallant keeps it.

He forces the Doctor to take him to the bridge of the flagship. There he overwhelms the Commander and his two aides and gains control of the Kyben spaceship.

"Now I'll do my duty," he tells Willie. She thinks he means to thwart the aliens, and her opinion of him has by now undergone a complete change. But she realizes he is acting strangely, not preparing to destroy the aliens. He tells Willie he wants the Commander to call in his men, to get them all together at once, to destroy the Kyben threat in one blow. If this huge flagship fails to rejoin its fleet, then the Kyben will have to fall back, give Earth time to prepare itself, muster its forces, defend itself in this sector of the galaxy.

Willie's suspicions are lulled. Tallant—using his dust-power over the Doctor—learns what signals must be given to call back all elements of the Kyben force. The signal is given, all flitters and scoutships return to the huge mother ship, the ports are sealed, all wait. What will Tallant do?

While Willie keeps the Doctor under guard on the bridge, Benno Tallant, with a portable translating machine, takes the Commander to his cabin. There he explains he has no loyalty left for the Earthmen who condemned him to die. He offers his aid in leading the Kyben fleet through the human outpost picket lines. The Kyben Commander accepts the offer, and Tallant tells him to get the rest of the Kyben fleet together. The Commander agrees.

When they return to the bridge, Tallant manages to get the blaster away from Willie, and reveals his plan. Her hatred of him leaps back into full force. She knew it all along...a dustie, a coward, a traitor...she tries to attack him, and he has her put in temporary stasis, awake, aware of what is happening, but frozen, floating in the air.

Finally, the fleet joins the Commander's flagship, and Tallant leads them toward Earth. When they reach the orbit of a dead world just outside the Solar System, Benno Tallant tells the Commander he wants to take his revenge on the girl, the only one of those who planted the bomb in him who won't be killed when the Kyben attack.

He takes her out in a two-man scoutship, and detaches half the cab, and sends her off into space, toward Earth, explaining that he has no affection for the men of Earth, nor for her, but neither has he any for the Kyben.

"What I am, I am, and I can't do anything about that. But if I was dirt before, at least Parkhurst and his boys taught me I'm a man, and that ties us all together," he explains.

Willie is sent away.

He takes his time getting back to the flagship, and to the other ships of the Kyben fleet, arrayed in ready battle formation on the dead, dark planetoid.

Back on the bridge, Tallant stalls for time. After several hours, estimating that Willie has had time to get out of the range of the blast area, he sets off the sun-bomb.

On her way in toward Earth, the viewscreen in Willie's scoutship bleeps and she turns it on. She asks for Parkhurst. They locate him, put him on, and when he asks what the great living ball of flame in space is, she tells him Benno Tallant carried out his mission more courageously than they had hoped.

And we close on the new star of light that the coward, the looter, the frightened Benno Tallant had become. We hold on the leaping flames and

FADE OUT.

The Darkness
Behind Their Eyes

The Alfred Hitchcock Hour (ca. 1962–1963)

Set back in a secluded California coast valley, the Black Leaf School, founded in 1915, today possesses an unblemished reputation as one of the finest private schools for boys and girls. Catering to the needs of the wealthy, the Black Leaf School boasts children from the homes of judges, senators, motion picture stars, and millionaires, sent to this fabulous educational institution whose brochure promises preparation for life, teaching capacities far superior to public schools, and a social life second to none.

This is what the brochure promises.

Hannah Kellogg comes to the Black Leaf School after two years of widowed sadness and loneliness. At 38, an attractive and sensitive woman, Hannah married young and was never compelled to pick up the secretarial skills employed by most women who must, finally, support themselves. Having been interviewed by mail, Hannah has been offered a six-month contract as a house mother; the lush surroundings, the tennis courts, stables, the happy children, the opulence of this highly-respected private school seem precisely the atmosphere she needs to wash away the emptiness of the past two years; and though the pay is inordinately low, still it is all clear, for room and board are furnished and what she makes she can keep.

Her correspondence with Dr. Leonard Fell, headmaster of Black Leaf, has been mutually exciting, and now as she meets him and hears him speak of the impressive job the school is doing with its charges, she knows she has made up her mind. She accepts the position as Fell assures her, "You'll come to think of Black Leaf as home. We're just a quiet country school, set among rolling hills."

That's what the brochure promises...

And just outside Fell's office window, a face. A boy's face. A small boy with strange eyes and a peculiar twist to his mouth. Alert. Listening. As his friends play, he stands outside the window, laughing with them, but distant, listening carefully to what Hannah Kellogg says, and softly, strangely, he smiles.

Dr. Fell rings for Paula Williams, a teacher in the school, who has been substituting as house mother in the dorm Hannah will oversee. Fell tells Hannah that it is very nearly dinnertime, and that Miss Williams will walk her over to her dorm, introduce her to the boys she will be in charge of, and then she should come down to dinner.

As they pace across the spacious grounds, Hannah is oddly disquieted at Paula Williams's bitter replies to her questions. She decides Paula is not very sensitive, and vows she will be more friendly to the children than the younger woman.

When they reach the dorm, Hannah is introduced to her charges, and in particular to Eric and Brian. Eric, we see, is the peculiar boy who was eavesdropping through Fell's window, and on closer scrutiny the mysterious quality of his face and manner register clearly. Brian is the son of a senator and seems to have stepped directly out of a Norman Rockwell cover. Clean, straight, decent, he seems the opposite of Eric, yet it is apparent they are close friends.

Paula Williams excuses herself and leaves, instructing the boys to help Hannah with her bags. Eric and Brian volunteer hurriedly, at Eric's insistence. They carry Hannah's bags to her room, and Brian excuses himself, saying he is going down to dinner. Eric stays on with Hannah as she begins hanging up her clothes, and he touches one of her dresses hesitantly, almost reverently, saying, "This is a lovely dress, Mrs. Kellogg. I like you, I really like you. You aren't like that Mrs. Cutler who was here before you. She was always mean and spying on us. But you're nice, I like you very much. And these are *such* pretty dresses; you're so beautiful."

His peculiar tone makes Hannah Kellogg pause in her labors to appraise him more closely. A friendly child, this ten-year-old. Yet there is something so odd, so pathetic and demanding of affection, that she senses at once there is more to him than merely adolescent peculiarity.

She goes down to dinner after Eric has left, and is impressed to see all the boys in dark suits, French cuff shirts, ties and brightly scrubbed.

At the dinner table Eric manages to sit next to Hannah, and a very small incident—Eric wrenching a serving tray from another boy, offering the food to Hannah himself—further focuses the boy in her mind.

That night Hannah goes to bed, but lies awake listening to music on her clock-radio, staring at a framed photograph of her dead husband, and hearing the sound of the hills outside. As she lies there, another sound comes to her, the sound of crying. She rises, slips into a robe and slippers, and goes outside; following the sound of voices and crying, she comes to the frog pond, and in the shadows she sees a group of boys and girls deeply involved in some sort of activity.

When she startles them with her voice, they break and scatter, leaving one of their group behind. Hannah comes closer and finds a young girl—perhaps eleven—tied to one of the huge stone benches surrounding the frog pond, crying piteously. She unties the girl and extracts the hysterical information that a secret society initiation was in progress, and they were trying to get the girl to eat a live frog.

Hannah asks who was behind it, but the little girl will not answer, terrified. Hannah sends the girl back to the dorm from which she has sneaked-away, and as she starts to return to her own building she hears soft laughter from the bushes. But when she investigates, finds no one.

The next day Paula Williams takes Hannah on a tour of the school, and in a brief series of vignette-segué-vignette scenes with dialogue, we learn of the school's high reputation, the fact that all of these children come from wealthy families—sons and daughters of those too important to care about the day-to-day needs of their children—and that each child who boards in owns his own horse, that it costs thirteen hundred dollars per year to maintain a child in the school, and other data about the mechanics of the school.

Hannah asks about Eric and Brian. Paula Williams manages to avoid the question, pointing to a handsome library building: "Half the money for that building came from Eric's mother, Adela George, the actress."

"But he's a rather strange little boy," Hannah says. "Has the school psychiatrist talked to him?"

Paula smiles enigmatically. "*What* psychiatrist...?"

Later that afternoon, Hannah comes into the dorm to find Eric playing with broken picture-frame glass. "You'd better give me that, Eric," she says, seeing one long shard that Eric seems to be fancying. She puts out her hand, but Eric pulls back, will not give it to her. When she tries to force him, he lunges at her, and in fear Hannah backs away from him. She threatens to go to Dr. Fell and tell him; Eric sneers, tells her to do it. He lunges at her again with the shard of glass, and Hannah, fearing the little boy may strike upward and blind her, rushes off to find Fell. As she races through the halls, Paula Williams stops her. When she tells Paula what is happening, the woman advises her to forget it, to leave the matter alone.

Hannah is incredulous, briefly castigates Paula for her callousness, says she will never wind up the way the other woman has, that she must stop Eric before he hurts himself. Paula shrugs, and Hannah rushes to Fell with the story.

She is appalled and amazed when Fell says, "We let the children have whatever playthings they want, until they cause trouble with it."

"Broken glass? Why not a shotgun, a hand grenade!"

Fell smiles benignly. "Mrs. Kellogg, we believe in letting the children learn from experience. If you feel Eric is playing with something dangerous, then why not take it away from him?"

Hannah explains her fear, and Fell makes light of it. She cannot understand his cavalier attitude. She presses the point...

...meanwhile Eric has gone to the dispensary and asked the nurse for some adhesive tape. Without bothering to find out what he wants it for, the nurse gives it to Eric, and the boy makes a handle of tape around the needle of glass.

Hannah has made such a storm, in the meantime, that Fell sends for Eric. When the boy comes in, Fell asks him for the weapon, and the boy hands it over. The doctor says, "we aren't going to play with glass anymore, are we, Eric?" The boy says no, he won't, and shakes hands with the head master. Then he leaves, giving Hannah a deadly look.

Fell soothes Hannah, saying, "There, now, wasn't that simple? All we had to do was allow the boy to make his own decision, treat him like a responsible person, and he came right through, didn't he?" Hannah reluctantly agrees, but she is upset, disturbed.

Back in the dorm, Hannah finds Eric in her room; as she walks in, Eric lifts the picture of her husband, and dashes it to the floor. Hannah stares, speechless, as Eric, crying, says: "No, I'll never play with picture glass again. I hate you!"

He runs out, and Hannah sinks down on the edge of the bed, shattered a bit herself. What has she gotten herself into?

As the days pass, Hannah becomes closer to Brian and Eric, finds Brian a quick and clever boy with respect and decency ingrained in his makeup, and with an added dimension: sympathy and deep friendship for Eric. But the latter is that free sort of spirit that knows no restraint, no discipline, and a brutalized sort of adolescence that carries, seemingly, its own destruction and depravity.

She finds that Eric, and several other boys—apparently problem children—do not attend their classes if they don't want to, that they are then signed in for "remedial teaching" at eight dollars an hour. She sits in on one of these supplemental classes, and finds they are almost worthless, that the children are treated with a *laissez-faire* attitude that only sends them back to the extra class (at $8 per hour) for more work. When she confronts one of the teachers with the seeming incompetence of the system, she is rebuffed, and told, "These little monsters don't want to learn, and their parent don't care if they *do* learn. We concentrate on feeding them the right answers to college entrance exams, that's all they need, all their families want, the stature of their child going to college. And if it weren't for the extra money we make with these additional classes, believe me, none of us would stay on here and put up with the agony we're put through."

Hannah has begun to suspect the corruption that lies just beneath the glossy surface of the school, and this merely reinforces her convictions. She is summoned to Fell's office for a talk, and in his severe tone she detects fear and cowardice as he tries to explain why her questions and suspicions are ill-founded, troublesome, annoying. And in their conversation she realizes just how corrupt the School actually is. Fell inevitably commands her to stop prying, or suffer dismissal. Hannah subsides, more out of discretion than fear or acquiescence.

Hannah's choices are plain: she may leave the school, and ignore what she knows is happening there, or she may stay on and assume the same calloused disposition of the other teachers and dorm mothers, or she can place herself in the center of the problem by trying to help the children, by getting next to them, trying to befriend them.

She makes tentative overtures to Eric and Brian—the latter of whom has become cold toward her, obviously due to Eric's feelings—and is rebuffed. She suggests to Fell that she take the boys of her dorm to the zoo, for an outing, and though Fell is wary, she convinces him, and they go.

At the zoo, Hannah tries to warm Eric and Brian to her confidence, but Eric still chills her; Brian, on the other hand, decides he and Hannah can be friends, and they discuss Eric. Brian tells Hannah that when Eric's mother—the actress—brought Eric to the school six months before, she literally dropped him in the driveway with his bags, tossed him a perfunctory, "Now you better be a good boy!" and drove away. He tells her he knows Eric does bad things, but he is his friend. "He doesn't have a father, Miz Kellogg, and he's always so sad 'n' unhappy, he needs me for his friend." Hannah is moved to compassion, not only for Eric, but for this decent boy whose empathy had been so much richer than her own. "Well, from now on, Brian," Hannah assures him, "we'll both be Eric's friends."

And then they hear the screams, the shrieks of maddened animals, and Hannah leaps up, follows the sound, to find Eric—a sharp stick in his hands—tormenting the lions. When she tries to drag him away, he strikes at her with the stick, becomes psychopathic, thrashes about, screams, hurls himself back at the cage, and finally...collapses.

Hannah wants to take Eric to a nearby clinic, but Paula, who had accompanied the group, insists that they return to the school. Hannah argues that Eric needs immediate attention, but Paula stops her with the harsh truth that, "one drop of publicity about this, one word getting back, and we could both be out of jobs."

"What's so wrong with that?" Hannah snarls, anger flaming in her. "You've been so hardened you think more of your job than what happens to this boy!"

"I've been at Black Leaf ten years, Hannah. I've seen dozens of other teachers and dorm mothers butter up these children, get close to them, keep writing to their parents so they'll inevitably get a position as a governess or tutor at their mansion. Security, Hannah. Security! I've been here ten years, and when I first came I was like you. But they don't want to cure their children...they don't want them at home...they want them here, where someone else will deal with the problems. Ten years, Hannah. Fell would fire us both...we have to take Eric *back*!"

Hannah examines Eric, decides he can be moved, and partially shocked into agreement by Paula's desperation, returns to Black Leaf with her charges, Brian tending watch over his comatose friend.

When they return, Hannah takes Eric to the infirmary, where the school nurse takes over. Hannah makes the remark as she leaves Eric that the nurse might take better care of him than the time she gave him the tape, without asking what it was for. The nurse, a hard-bitten and burly woman, warns Hannah that her prying and arrogant attitude will cause her trouble. This threat, barely veiled, is delivered in such surly tones, that Hannah seeks out Paula Williams once more, and badgers her into revealing just what is wrong with the school.

"This isn't like a public school, where the staff has to be responsible to a board of education, and thus to the people. This is a privately-endowed school, and Fell is the only law here. It started out as a highly-reputable place, but after a while, children with problems who had been dropped out of other private schools came here, and Fell accepted the first one, then another, without the sort of screening that keeps these disturbed children out of the pack, and under special psychiatric care. After a while, word got around in the loftier social circles, and every warped or neurotic child a wealthy family didn't want around to stigmatize their good name, wound up here."

Hannah is incredulous. "There are more like Eric?"

"More? Hannah, we have bed-wetters here, we have children who are sixteen years old and can't read, we have little boys who are more female than male, we have one child who is a pathological thief...but only of things that other children want."

Hannah finds this chamber of horrors too unbelievable to accept. "But why does Fell continue to accept them, why doesn't he expel them?"

"Endowments, gifts. The silent deals that are made, Hannah. A new building for the library, if a child remains on the roles here, so his mother can say, 'Yes, my son is up at Black Leaf, and doing wonderfully well.' And the teachers, myself included, Hannah, we need the gifts, the little tokens of esteem the families send us, the summer jobs, the gratuities. A woman can feather her nest very nicely if she's clever and quick, here."

"But they can't all be that way here, Paula. Some of these children must be healthy, good students."

Paula nods. "Of course. There is a certain larger proportion of children who are perfectly acceptable in any school. They've been sent here by parents who've been duped by the brochure. And you can't see the evil here just by looking at the stables or the classrooms or the olympic-sized swimming pool. But the good ones don't stay long. They move on."

"Why don't the children write home and complain about the strange goings-on?" Hannah asks.

"Why? I'll show you why," Paula says, stopping in front of a classroom. "Sit down in the back of the room and listen."

Hannah sits in on the English class, and hears the children being forced to read their letters home aloud. To the class. And derogatory remarks or reports of odd happenings are stricken-out by the instructor.

Hannah leaves the classroom, appalled at what she has learned, determined to do something. But what?

Back in her dorm, Hannah is confronted by Brian. The boy is concerned for his friend Eric. Hannah says she will take Brian to the infirmary to see him, but when they get there, the nurse will not allow them to enter. They go away, Hannah frightened and concerned.

That evening, Brian comes to Hannah and says the nurse has gone into town with her boyfriend, that the infirmary is untended. Hannah cannot believe this, but she goes with Brian to the place where Eric is being kept. She finds him, and several other children, apparently sleeping. But when Brian tries to waken him, they discover that the ten-year-old has been put under heavy sedation.

As incredible as this seems, Hannah removes the boy to his dorm, instructs Brian and several others to keep watch over him, and goes to see Fell once more.

The headmaster is furious at Hannah's discoveries, tries to placate her, but she demands that Eric be expelled for his own good. That his mother must be forcibly made aware of his dire emotional state, and that it is necessary for the good of the other boys. Fell refuses. There is too much money at stake. Hannah curses him, calling him a coward and a corrupter of children. Fell tells her she is through at the School. Hannah snaps back, "I have a six month contract, and I'm staying on, Dr. Fell...and the only way you'll get me out of that contract is to take me to court. How would *that* sit with your all-important board of trustees, and the families of these children?"

Fell is backed into a corner. He cannot get rid of this woman, nor can he discredit her. He must bide his time. That night Eric is returned to the infirmary.

The days pass, and Eric—after nearly a week of constant sedation—is returned to his dorm and though dull and slow, seems recovered. He tries to stage another frog-eating induction, but is stopped by Brian.

Hannah talks to Brian, tries to convince him that Eric needs help he cannot get here, and that he must write to his father, the senator, asking him to come down to the Alumni Carnival the following month. She says she will smuggle out the letter. Brian agrees.

The month passes with several sharp incidents to mark Eric's schizoid conduct, and his worsening state. Hannah's dresses are slashed...a little girl who defied Eric meets with a near-fatal accident in the swimming pool...Fell turns his back on the scene, saying only if a federal law is broken can he expel a student.

Then comes the Carnival, and Brian's father meets Hannah. They strike an immediate rapport, and when she tells him of the true nature of the place, he is at first amazed, disbelieving, then incredulous. He says he will have to speak to the headmaster about this. Hannah knows, of course, that this means her job, that now her overt act of defiance to Fell and the school means her dismissal.

As they eat dinner in the huge dormitory dining room, upstairs, Eric is preparing another of his "pranks." He has filled several dozen paraffin-candy bottles (the penny kind containing sweet-flavored colored juice, the kind children buy in candy stores) with rubbing alcohol. He has given these to his fellow students, and they have become slightly ill. Ill enough to allow Eric to take a straight razor and shave their heads, all but for Sioux-style hairlocks. Then he marches them down into dinner, a weird, Kafkaesque scene—the boys in their smart, dark suits, ties, white shirts with French cuffs...and shaved heads.

Brian's father is convinced. He goes to Fell, tells him he wants Brian's records, he is removing the boy from the school, and there will be an investigation, if *he* has anything to say about it.

Hannah packs as Brian packs. The boy is disconsolate. His friend Eric remains in Black Leaf. They pause in the front hall, waiting for Brian's father to come with the car, and Hannah tries to explain to Brian that it is a good thing for him to leave, that a good boy, thrown in a barrel of rotten apples, must surely be corrupted himself. He cannot understand.

"Brian, this school isn't typical. There are only a half dozen or so like it in the country. Most private schools are fine places, and your father will send you to one of them. As for Black Leaf, I'm not sure an investigation will do any good. There's really nothing to uncover but sickness, and that isn't criminal. But perhaps enough publicity will make itself felt, and even Eric's mother will see what she's done to her child.

"The blame isn't with the children, God knows, Brian. It's with these creatures, Fell and his teachers, who feed off their illness and get fat off it. But mostly it's all those mothers and fathers who are too rich or too busy or too uninterested to care what happens to their children. And perhaps all this will open their eyes, because this is something that is happening today, right now, Brian, and people have to learn about it before they can correct it."

Brian's father pulls up in the car and Hannah and the boy get into it, as we cut to Eric, his face still at the window as it was when first we saw him, looking out this time, watching his friends drive away.

And we close on the little boy, crying, staring in loneliness and the fear of his own disturbed nature, from the window that has become his prison.

Mrs. Pigsfoot

Honey West (19 May 1965)

TEASER:

Handsome BENJY CASIMIR stole a quarter of a million dollars from a small California bank (monthly payroll for the big aircraft plant nearby). And he did seventeen years in prison for it. But they never found the two hundred and fifty thousand. Now, as we FADE IN, we see Benjy being released. The law is like that; sometimes it's vindictive as hell, other times it throws up its hands and says, "Let him go, maybe we'll drop lucky one of these mornings, and Benjy Casimir'll come in with a fistful of money." But nobody's making book on it; Benjy ain't the type.

So, Benjy walks out of State Prison, carrying his little suitcase, and sitting in a convertible outside the gate is one of the longest-legged, smooth-skinned, honey blonde cupcakes anyone could imagine. And after seventeen years of enforced abstinence, Benjy is the best imaginer imaginable. The vision swings open the door of the car, smiles a smile of purple velvet and says, "Hi, Benjy, I've been waiting for you." Benjy stares, but walks to her.

"Who're you?"

"I'm Micki Riley," she says. "My older sister was IRIS RILEY. You remember, the teller at the bank you robbed—the one who helped you get that quarter of a million. Iris is gone, but I grew up. Hop in."

Benjy stares. So do we. That girl isn't MICKI RILEY...

It's HONEY WEST.

Benjy slides into the car, throws his suitcase in back, Honey smiles at him, and as she is about to drop the convertible into drive, suddenly a LITTLE OLD LADY appears from nowhere, dressed in a long old-fashioned Dame May Whitty dress, with high-button shoes, pale white hair piled at the nape of her neck in a bun, with old-fashioned steel-rim glasses on her wrinkled face, and pushing a shopping cart loaded with groceries. We come in CLOSE on her, and see her squinting myopically at Benjy and Honey. Then she abruptly pulls a large target pistol from her grocery bag, aims, and fires, and a great round shock-concussion circle appears in the windshield, CLOSE ON IT and HONEY'S FACE wide-eyed behind it as we HARD CUT TO the face of the little old lady and ZOOM IN RAPIDLY on her myopic eye, behind the round eyeglass as we IRIS-SPIRAL out of the blinking eye TO:

MAIN TITLES

ACT ONE:

REVERSE IRIS-SPIRAL into a CLOSEUP of shattered glass on the windshield of the convertible. Honey and Benjy Casimir are in a garage, getting the glass repaired. Honey excuses herself to freshen her makeup. In the women's john, she speaks to SAM BOLT over her lipstick transmitter.

Through their brief conversation, we learn that Honey has been hired by the Insurance Company to track down the money and they have given Honey dossiers on Benjy and Iris Riley. They are sure that left to his own devices, Benjy will quickly lose himself to pursuers, grab the cached quarter of a million (wherever it is, having eluded discovery for seventeen years), cut-and-run, then away to Brazil for a lifetime of goodies, having only given up seventeen years in a warm cell...which isn't a bad exchange, when you stop to think that most people waste their lives in quiet desperation chained to lives of drudgery and boredom and never even come anywhere *near* a quarter of a million dollars.

Sam is trailing Honey in the truck, a remote control bleeper secreted in the rear fender bumper guard, and he warns her that even though he is right behind, not to take any chances, there are obviously others out to get Benjy and/or the loot. Honey remembers the old lady and that shot through the windshield; she agrees with Sam.

But, she reminds him, her position with Casimir himself is an ideal one: when Benjy was arrested, his accomplice, young and beautiful Iris Riley had vanished (there was some conjecture that if they ever found the money, they would find the moldering frame of Iris keeping it company) and the Insurance Company had been approached by Micki Riley, within the past year, to help them bring Casimir to justice. Micki feels Benjy did in her sister, and her desire for revenge has taken the form of letting Honey pose as the other Riley girl, to entice Benjy.

Honey has rightfully reasoned that the only stranger Benjy could tolerate within grabbing distance, would be an extraordinarily beautiful woman, after his long term in stir. Type-casting, you might say.

As they discuss the moves for lulling Benjy's suspicions—and staying out of shotgun range of old ladies—Honey hears a sound outside the rest room, and suddenly throwing it open, she tackles a man who was eavesdropping. She fells him, only to have him plead that he is on her side. She lets him up, drags him around the back of the station where Benjy won't see them, and find it is LIONEL C. PERTWEE, the regular insurance operative on the case, a mild and mildewy ribbon clerk of a man who is upset that after seventeen years on the dossier, the company has seen fit to bring in someone else, right when Pertwee feels he has the case in the palm of his hands. And a *woman*, at that! Well!

Honey warns Pertwee to stay out of the way, that she is close to the matter now, and he can only snafu it by interfering. Pertwee is insulted, and stalks off into the tall grass, to skulk about some more.

Honey gazes heavenward, then quickly tells Sam about Pertwee, advises Sam to keep an eye on the little man, just to keep him from throwing any Stillson wrenches into the cams, gears, and cogs of her masquerade. She returns to Benjy, does a little bill and coo *shtick*, and they take off, as Pertwee peers after them, from the bushes. Then he pulls down his goggles, kicks his cycle, and takes off after them in a baroooom and a cloud of smoke, bowler, attaché case, and all.

As they near the town where the robbery first took place, suddenly a long, black limousine pulls abreast of them, starts firing at the tires with a machine gun, and they are run off the road. Benjy goes over the open top and lands in a thicket, unconscious.

Three charcoal-gray hoods, looking like business executives, pop out of the limousine and start for the convertible, when Honey lets loose with her own revolver. They are scared away, just as Sam pulls up, Pertwee in tow.

"Who the hell were *they*!?!" Sam wants to know. "This is about as secret a maneuver as a 4th of July picnic!"

Pertwee opines the three gunsels were dispatched by GEORGE-O KRULNIK, downstate boss of the slot machine/juke-box/horse parlor combine that (it was rumored at the time of the trial) was the original mastermind of the bank robbery. Benjy, Pertwee suggests, crossed his combine friends, skipped with the loot, and then protected himself by getting sent up the river for a safe, prolonged period. Honey and Sam boggle.

Then Honey realizes Benjy is going to come to at any moment, so she hustles Sam off, towing the squirming Pertwee. She goes to Benjy, cradles his bowed but unbroken head in her lap, and listens as he mumbles the name "Mrs. Pigsfoot...Mrs. Pigsfoot's got it..." Is this a clue to the whereabouts of the money?

When Benjy comes around, he is terrified, saying George-O is out to get him...that he suspected it when the old lady sniped at them...but he recognized the three hoods as being George-O's contract hit men.

He asks what happened to them, and Honey lies that they didn't see the car go off the road, and kept going. Benjy looks dubious, but seeing no long, black limousine, he accepts the story.

They get back into the convertible as we SMASH CUT TO another garage, where they are having the car repaired, just as The Little Old Lady tries again. This time with a bow and arrow. The shaft doesn't look very decorative, sunk through Honey's new picture hat, anchoring it to the wall of the garage.

ACT TWO:

They arrive in the town, get a motel room. Benjy tries some hanky and/or panky with Honey, and in a fit of girlish pique (staying in character as Micki) she slaps Benjy's face which we MATCH CUT TO:

George-O Krulnik slapping the face of Shadrack, Meshack, and Kupperman, who offers as their excuses a number of graphs, time-motion studies, tables of odds regulating success, and a group of bullet holes in their clothing from the leggy blonde protecting Benjy whilst he lay asleep on the sward. George-O is not amused. He tells them to get that broad outta the way, she is obviously engaged in what is commonly referred to by the hoi and the polloi as no good. They salute, and off to errand they go.

Casimir, bugged at Honey's refusal to cooperate in a project he has waited seventeen years to consummate, tells her he has an "errand" to run, and he will be back. Honey quickly calls Sam, and tells him to tail Benjy, mentioning the Mrs. Pigsfoot clue.

Honey decides to check over the town, see if she can get a line on the Little Old Lady. She talks to several shopkeepers who reminisce about the robbery, but all they know is that poor Iris Riley was murdered, sure enough.

Honey realizes she is herself being shadowed, and in establishing that it is George-O's three heavies coming for her, she ducks down an alley, over a fence, through a beauty salon, and comes out on a side street right in front of a little jam & jelly shop with a sign that proclaims

MOTHER MARTHA'S FAMOUS PIGSFOOT JELLY
Finest Jams & Preserves This Side Of
Where The Woodbine Twineth

Hoo-*ha*! Honey enters the shop through the front door, hears two voices in the back, and peering through the curtain sees Benjy Casimir talking to The Little Old Lady, none other than MOTHER MARTHA herself. She throws down on them when she hears Mother Martha say that the money has been taken out of her savings account, and that they have not only the quarter of a million, but all the interest it has accrued over seventeen years.

However...

George-O and his boys intrude, and throw down on *them*, telling Benjy and Honey and Mother Martha that they will shortly be residing at the bottom of Round Schooner Lake, a hundred and forty-six miles upstate, now that they know the money is hereabouts.

However...

Lionel C. Pertwee intrudes, and throws down on *them*, telling Benjy and Honey and Mother Martha and George-O and Shadrack, Meshack & Kupperman that he hasn't been so hot on the trail because he wanted to solve it for the insurance company; he has been hot on the trail for seventeen years because he has worked like a dray-horse for the company, and when he retires he wants more than a gold watch and a testimonial dinner, so he will kill all seven of them, thank you very much for the idea of Round Schooner Lake, and mix enough cement for seven instead of merely three, it's only sand and water, after all.

However...

Sam Bolt intrudes and throws down on the entire pack of them, and Honey and Sam truss up the group, with the exception of the kindly little old lady who, divested of her target pistol, bow, and arrow, is really rather harmless. They try to get her to tell them where the money is, for consideration with the authorities, and Mother Martha agrees.

However...

She produces a gun and throws down on Sam and Honey, and trusses them. The total to be dispensed with now reaches the staggering total of nine, and George-O laughs aloud. A little old lady like that, killing nine people...ridiculous!

However...

À la *From Russia, with Love*, Mother Martha strips away the makeup of an old woman, slips out of the Victorian garb, and wearing a bikini (which is the only logical thing to wear under such a hot heat-producing disguise) she reveals herself to be not a seventy-year-old hag, but curvaceous, gorgeous woman.

"How about Iris Riley," she smiles at George-O, "do you think she's able enough to take care of the nine of you? Sound of hoof and fetlock, friend, no problem at all."

Startlement, chagrin, horror, and frustration are a few of the do-it-yourself expressions the small but tidy group registers, as Iris produces a silencer from a drawer, and prepares for a second Valentine's Day Massacre.

TAG:

"But why me, too!?!" shrieks Benjy Casimir.

"Listen, Benjy Casimir," Iris Riley snaps, "seventeen years ago you had a real banana here. I was so green I didn't realize I was about to spend the best years of my life posing as an old lady, so I could slip that money into a savings account little by little, so we could get all the interest on it, and leading a life of real yechhhh! with only a weekend in Los Angeles from time to time. Maybe seventeen years ago I would've gone for it, but it's been a long, lonely seventeen, friend, and if you think I like coming to meet you at the prison to find you with this... this...phoney blonde...you're sadly mistaken..."

Honey gets to her feet. Only her hands are tied, behind her back. "Phoney blonde!" She starts toward Iris. Iris waves the gun menacingly. "Get back, tootie, I'll use you for a dartboard." Honey grins, "You won't shoot!" Sam yells for Honey to stop it, not to encourage Iris, but Honey keeps coming, and suddenly lashes out with a karate *savate* kick that sends Iris backwards, halfway across the room, as her wild shot blows a huge jar of parsnip marmalade off the wall.

Then Honey has to find a way to get her bonds off. She knocks a jar of pigsfoot jelly off the shelf, to use the glass to cut the ropes, but when Sam stoops to pick up the glass, to work on Honey's bonds, he sees the jar didn't contain pigsfoot jelly at all. A quarter of a million dollars + interest, neatly rolled, rubber-banded, and hidden in dark glass jars.

Later, they wend their way through a report of the caper and Honey acknowledges Benjy and Iris's cleverness in having her disappear, letting everyone think she was dead (knowing without a corpus no murder charges could be brought against Benjy), and then having her return, disguised, to the last place anyone would think to look for her, the town where they'd committed the robbery. And what better hideaway for the money than the very bank from which it had been stolen.

"But why did you take such a chance walking against her gun?" Sam wants to know, exasperated with Honey's recklessness.

Honey grins. "Who was worried. A woman who carries off such a thorough disguise as that couldn't afford to wear phoney glasses. Her eyesight must have been lousy...when she took off the glasses I was sure she couldn't hit a barn from the inside."

Close in on Honey's eyes, as we did the old lady's much earlier, and we realize she was a classic case of astigmatism. Spiral-iris and we

FADE OUT:

THE END

In the Valley of the Winds

Amos Burke, Secret Agent (25 May 1965)

TEASER:

FADE IN London. Long shot of Big Ben or similar clock tower. Yet this is not the typical establishing shot of that famous clock, for as we MOVE IN RAPIDLY we ZOOM THRU the face of the clock with its hands at three minutes to midnight and see the reverse side of the clock, the huge, hollow, and shadowed, echoing mechanism chamber, stretching up into eerie darkness, and the two gigantic crossbeams that anchor the hands of the clock from the opposite side. They, too, are poised at three minutes to midnight. But now we see that a man is securely tied to the hour hand, already straight up. And as the matching beam, the one anchoring the minute hand, crosses over the hour hand, the prisoner on that clock will be steadily and mercilessly crushed to death. The man is sweating, as we hear a no-nonsense voice out of the darkness: "You have exactly two minutes to live. Tell me where you've lured the girl to meet you."

The voice of AMOS BURKE. He steps out of the shadows, and we see his handsome face set in lines of determination. He obviously dislikes what he is forced to do to this man, but the situation seems incredibly tense...and as the moments pass, and the great clockwork mechanism above and around them chitters mechanically, we see the prisoner on the beam sweat. "I'll never tell. You can kill me, but you'll never learn."

"When that minute hand says 12:00 straight up," Burke replies, "it all becomes academic. Then I blow this case, I get a reprimand from my superiors, and I go out on another job. None of which helps you."

As the minute hand closes, the man finally cracks. He tells Burke the girl has been lured to the warehouse district of Soho by agents of his government (which we understand by his accent to be operatives of the USSR) on the pretext that she will be contacted by an American.

Burke cuts him loose.

As the man is released, he suddenly springs cat-like, to the side, and in CLOSEUP we see a switchblade attached to a spring-driven mechanism, shoot out of his sleeve, and into his hand. He comes for Burke in a trained street-fighter's crouch, slashing upward. Burke leaps back as the blade rips open the front of his smoothly-tailored jacket. The assassin moves in again, and they tussle. The open crenelations of the clock tower are all around them, looking down on empty air and a sheer drop to the street below. They fight, and suddenly the assassin kicks out at Burke. Amos grabs the man's foot with both of his, and cupping it, hurls him up and back. The man falls, screaming, from the bell tower, which we see in MED LONG SHOT from the street and then

ZOOM IN on the clock face again as the clock slowly, carefully begins striking midnight.

FADE OUT.

ACT ONE:
    FADE IN a CLOSEUP on Burke, standing at a curbside all-night fish 'n' chips stand in the rundown warehouse section of Soho. As we hold on him, a man carrying a thin cabretta-grain attaché case, and wearing a bowler hat, passes him, enters a building across the way. We see him, note him, but do not linger on him.

Burke suddenly sees the girl riding up the street toward him on a Lambretta motor scooter. She is quite lovely, young (25), and wears a trench coat that parted, shows a handsome stretch of leg as she rides the scooter. She gets off the Lambretta and cautiously starts walking up the street toward Burke, looking around as though trying to ascertain if this is a trap.

SMASH CUT to a shot through a warehouse window, showing us the girl walking up the street toward Burke, as a bowler hat is laid on the window ledge, and we HOLD CLOSE on a pair of hands, wearing surgical rubber gloves, as they open the attaché case on the ledge, and begin assembling a breakaway sniper's rifle (similar to the weapon used in *From Russia, with Love*: a rimfire, semi-automatic .22 made by ArmaLite, division of Fairchild Aircraft Corp.; author humbly offers his own weapon for this purpose, if needed).

Back down in the street, as Burke steps toward the girl, a huge black limousine suddenly flips on its lights, and roars out of the shadows of an alley where it has been all this time, unseen even by Burke. The limousine is obviously there to kidnap the girl. It plunges toward her.

As it passes him, he drops to one knee, fast-drawing his automatic, and steadying his hand across his knee, he fires a full clip into the tires. A tire blows, the limousine plunges sidewise and plows into a lamppost.

Burke streaks for the girl, starts to grab her before the kidnappers in the car can recover. Then we discover why the man in the bowler hat was added to this maneuver—as a safeguard, as an additional security measure, in case of American Intelligence interference. He opens up on Burke from the window as we SHOOT THRU WINDOW down on Amos throwing himself flat, palming another clip into the automatic, and lying prone, firing up into the window. He shoots the sniper out of the window, grabs the girl, and they escape.

Later, Amos is secreted with the girl in her flat in Cheltenham Mews. Her name is ELKE LOSCH. Her father was a Nazi bacteriological scientist. He has been missing for over twenty years, since the Allies overran the bacteriophage labs attached to Hitler's funeral bunker in Berlin, where he was working to create a super-weapon that might save the Third Reich at the eleventh hour.

She has been brought up in orphanages throughout Europe, she tells Burke, and had never heard of her father again, save that he had been killed at the same time Hitler had been killed. But mysteriously, on her twenty-fifth birthday, a few days before, a strange Asian had brought her a message, purportedly from her father, advising her that he was not only alive and well, but that his secret weapon had been perfected. The note further said that he wanted her to come to him to get this "secret" as her inheritance, all he had left to give her. She had known she would have to sell the secret to one or another government, and had contacted the

Americans for help. But the Communists had intercepted the message, and had tried to capture her, to get the weapon for their team. She had escaped, and hidden out, and when she had been contacted by what she thought were the Americans, she had come to the warehouse district, where the Russians had been waiting to kidnap her, and sniper-kill any US agents trying to interfere. Burke adds that intelligence had been tipped to the maneuver, and he had captured one of their operatives (as we have seen) and was able to intercede and save her at the last moment.

Now, together, they will find her father, HERR DOKTOR KONRAD LOSCH. She tells Amos that he is in a watertight bunker, in the silt and mud at the bottom of the Danube River, between the two cities that comprise Budapest.

Together they go to Budapest, and equipped with scuba gear, he prepares to dive into the river, leaving Elke as a lookout, in case of trouble. Bearing *plastique* to blow the bunker if he has to, Amos dives into the dark river as CAMERA PANS RIGHT and ZOOMS IN on three black-suited scuba divers watching from a hidden distance. They are Asian, with hard, Mongolian features, and they stare into the glowing screen of a strange little portable television set, on which we see the face of a memorable and mysterious figure, their superior, who is telling them to let the man dive, that they must know exactly how far Losch has gone with his treachery. He advises them to make sure the man does not come up, however, and we see the three assassins readying deadly spear-guns as we

FADE OUT.

ACT TWO:

Amos dives to the bunker. Carrying plastic explosives to blow it. He overpowers a guard. Guard is Asian. Burke is surprised, what is an Asian, obviously Mongolian, doing under the Danube in Budapest? He meets KONRAD LOSCH.

Losch is a weary old man, recognizes guilt for what he has allowed himself to be made to do. "Every man shares the guilt of all other men." All he wants to do is die, but he has been the prisoner—for twenty years—of the warlord of a small, obscure Asian country, who has practically bled his nation of every cent, to finance this project, with the final aim of establishing himself as a World Power. They have forced him to perfect his diabolical secret weapon. Losch's last act, he declares, must be to keep that weapon out of the hands of this unscrupulous mysterion, who intends only evil for the world.

The weapon: a mutated strain of anthrax, that blown on the wind, kills in a matter of minutes. Not only animals, but humans are unable to stand up to it; no treatment or preventative can be used. Once inhaled, it always ends terminally. (Based on recent scientific research into the anthrax spore-germs, as chronicled in the April 25th issue of *The New Yorker*.)

Losch tells Burke the canisters of poison spores have already been trans-shipped, going to a place he knows only as the Valley of the Winds. He begs Burke to kill him, to give him final peace, now that he has done what he can do to end this threat. He tells Burke that he was forced to work in Budapest, for the proper strains of bacteria for anthrax come from sheep hair, and the most virulent sort from Hungarian sheep.

Burke tries to tell Losch he still has much to live for, even if he is forced to stand trial for his crimes: he tells the scientist that his daughter got the message (Losch smiles softly at this; he had only this one thing he could do for the child he was forced to abandon so young; he had never really thought the message would get through with the bribed guard) and that she is well. He tells Losch the girl came with him and that she is on the chain bridge above the river, watching for the enemy.

Losch smiles, then his eyes widen. She's here? On the bridge? Watching...?

Burke assumes Losch's amazement is that his daughter is so near, but they don't have time to discuss it because the spy-eye that has been watching them all along (which we have seen, but have not recognized till now) relays a message to the three scuba assassins who have been waiting, and as their mysterious LEADER tells them to strike, that he knows all he needs to know at this point, they attack, and break in.

Burke has a vicious fight with them. Losch manages to save his life, but in the struggle is mortally wounded, Losch says he will hold them back while Burke plants the *plastique*.

As they are about to escape, Losch shoves Burke through the airlock, saying it is the only way, that he will have to stand the three assassins off till the explosive blows. He locks it before Burke can stop him, and though he tries to extricate the old man, he realizes it is futile as the seconds tick away. Finally, he starts to swim away.

There is a terrible explosion, which erupts on the surface of the Danube, where Elke Losch sees it. She hurries to make a rescue, as Burke, stunned by the concussion, floats to the surface unconscious.

There is a corpse boat (true) that runs between the cities of Buda and Pest. She commandeers it at gunpoint and rescues Amos, who floats to the surface still out cold. On the corpse boat they play the final scene of the act, in which Amos tells her that her father died to save her and the rest of the world from a terrible threat. But now, the most important thing is to find the enigmatic Valley of the Winds. And fast.

FADE OUT.

ACT THREE:

FADE IN Paris, backstage at the *Folies Bergère*. Burke's contact liaison is a showgirl in the chorus, a gigantic chorine over six feet tall (suggest Bea Bradley, formerly of *Stop the World—I Want to Get Off!*). She gives him his papers, passports, itinerary. The Intelligence Agency has located the mysterious Valley of the Winds: Burke will be heading for Tibet.

As Burke speaks to the girl in the wings, an old stooped lady, the wardrobe mistress, comes to them, and begins fussing with the leggy chorine's feathers, helping her adjust the Ziegfeld-style headdress. They let the talk lapse till the old woman wanders away, then they start again in a hushed tone, as we follow the old woman. She quickly mounts a flight of iron stairs, and in the catwalk above them, we see her pull off her hearing aid, and aim it down at the two people whispering below her. We hear them clearly, albeit on FILTER, and we realize it is a cunning directional microphone. We hear the liaison-chorine warn Burke that he is going against not one, but *two* enemies:

The men who rescued Konrad Losch from Berlin when the Allies came through, the cunning enemy who kept Losch in that bunker under the Danube for twenty years, the Asian leader who has sworn to make his tiny nation a third world power, even if it means the eradication of the two major powers already extant, the enemy whose intentions for the germ-spore weapon are still a mystery.

And the second enemy: the Communists who were the original interceptors of the Losch girl's communiqué with US Intelligence, who tried to kidnap her in London, whose sniper narrowly missed killing

Amos, as we have seen. She tells Burke there has been a security leak on the other side, and they now have definite information that the Russians have marked this operation top priority, and have assigned to it their top assassin, a shadowy figure known only as LE SAUVAGE—The Savage. This killer is responsible for over a dozen of the most infamous assassinations of the past ten years, a professional whose work is so coldly perfect, so devoid of emotion and involvement, that he has never even been seen, the agency has no "make" on him of any kind.

As Burke asks the girl what she can tell him of the Valley of the Winds, we see the old wardrobe mistress click on a tiny spy-eye tv transmitter, similar to the one used by the three scuba assassins in act two. The Leader is there, and he seems bemused by the conversation between Burke and the chorine. The wardrobe mistress holds up a rapier-thin air-gun (that fires a stream of deadly compressed air, capable of killing [true: such a weapon was found on the person of a gallery spectator at the Nuremberg War Crimes Trials, and as intended for undetected use from the audience, thereby causing the mysterious retributive deaths of Nazi war criminals] even from that height) but The Leader stops her. Let Burke go, he orders; he needs the Losch girl, and how much simpler it is for him if Burke brings her right to his doorstep. But the liaison must die.

The beautiful amazonian chorine advises Burke that he will be contacted in Tibet by a SHERPA HERDSMAN who had been the guest in the US of a senator (paralleling LBJ's camel driver from Afghanistan). She gives him necessary dossiers and files of what the Agency has been able to find out, and Burke leaves.

We HOLD on a LONG SHOT down on the backstage of the Follies, as we see Burke vanish through a stage door, the old wardrobe mistress level her weapon, a pftfft! of air, and far below the chorine clutches her forehead and topples. As the crowd begins screaming and milling about below us, the old woman vanishes into the shadows and we

BLUR-PAN through stock of the jetliner heading for the Himalayas and necessary linkage vignettes to match-meet Burke with the Sherpa herdsman, who takes him to his humble residence. There we see an amusing facet of international personal relations: the herdsman has been so impressed by America, that he is very slangy and Yankee-ized, in an attempt to emulate the land he finds so romantic and rewarding.

This is further borne out by our meeting with his four GORGEOUS DAUGHTERS, whom he has also Westernized, and for whom his sole ambition is that they go to the States, enter beauty contests and become Miss Americas, Miss Universes, etc.

These five become the commando task force for Burke and Elke Losch (who has insisted on coming along, saying that her father died for this weapon, that she might have it, and now, after all the years of impoverished orphan existence it is the only "inheritance" she has left; Burke relents). They will take the American and the girl to the Valley of the Winds.

And what is this Valley?

A legendary lost valley high in the Himalayas, part of an independent Chinese nation so small that it can seldom be found on maps of the world. A valley lost for most months of the year in snow so impassable and treacherous that approach by foot is impossible. A valley of such peculiar topographical properties that the winds of the Earth are literally born there where they converge, from whence they begin their journeys around the planet. A valley where the keening shriek of a million winds being born, returning to die in whispers, makes sound an impossibility, mere ear-plugs and communication by hand are necessities, save in the very center, where the "eye" of the wind-births causes a freakish silence of absolute permanence.

The Sherpa assures Burke that they are in luck. This is the summer of the Tibetan mountains, and though dangerous and rugged, they will be able to get through.

We take them through a MONTAGE of shots trekking to the Valley. There Burke caches the explosives he has brought to end the threat of the weapon. The seven of them peer over a snow-ridge and look down at the fantastic sight of the Valley. The screaming winds, whose intensity has steadily mounted till they reached this point, now overwhelm them, and even their ear-plugs don't seem capable of keeping out the roar of the mælstrom.

Yet their attention is held by the huge building which has been built in the cup of the valley. A strange black building around which the snow whirls, with great fan-like blowers on the roof. Burke looks at Elke, and we begin to understand what The Leader intends for that deadly anthrax spore. The plant is guarded by huge, towering Asian guards, the cream of a Mongolian warrior race, now clad as their ancestors, the hordes of Genghis Khan and Attila were clad, save equipped with automatic rifles and grenades.

Burke tells the four girls to return home, that he and their father and Elke will go it alone. The girls vanish into the snow and mist, and the three commandos move in on the plant, stealthily. At one point they enter the "eye" and are abruptly, eerily, surrounded by absolute silence...

We even see them moving in stealthily: on a spy-eye tv transmitter being watched by The Leader. He laughs. At last, his tardy guests have arrived. He signals for the trap to be sprung...

And as the three advance on the plant, suddenly molybdenum-steel spears spring from the ground, completely encircling them in a cage-like affair, with an opening at one end. And down through that opening lope a pack of slavering, rabid, trained white snow wolves, death in their eyes.

FADE OUT.

ACT FOUR:

They are in glass cells. Outside the cells the wolves roam hungrily. Finally, Burke is taken to see The Leader.

He is a tall, very thin and ascetic Asian, with a poetic bent. He is flowery, attentive, solicitous—and deadly. He sits behind a glass shield and tells Burke that he has not stood a chance of winning, all along, that he has been watched from the very start, that he has been allowed to find this hidden fortress, only because there was the need to know what Burke's agency suspected. And the girl. He tells Burke that for over twenty years his nation has been preparing for this day. That he has been forced to make the already-poor people of his tiny country live in abject poverty, so that every cent might be channeled into this project, a single gamble for world domination.

He assures Burke that it will be successful, for in just a few days, when the final mechanical preparations have been made with the anthrax spores, all communications media around the world will be jammed, and the visage of The Leader will appear on every tv set, every motion picture screen, his voice will be heard on every radio and wireless, at the same time, and he will make his demands:

World-wide blackmail. Using the strange and miraculous properties of the Valley of the Winds, he can literally blow the deadly anthrax to any pinpointed location in the world. He will tell the nations of the Earth that if each of them does not meet his demand of one billion dollars in gold bullion *each*, within 24 hours after his announcement, he will select three cities, and kill every living thing in them. He has selected Omsk in Russia, Rio de Janeiro, and to demonstrate that it matters not whether the target be large or small, Madison, Indiana, a tiny town in the USA.

Burke tries to rush the glass shield, but is overpowered and hurled back in his glass cage, to await a spare time when The Leader can interrogate him, using frightening Asian brainwashing techniques.

Two days later, The Leader goes on the air and makes his frightening demands. Then the 24-hour waiting period begins. During this time, The Leader decides to question Burke thoroughly, then dispose of him. But in the brainwashing room, a vast chamber filled half with implements of medieval torture, and half with scientific gadgetry calculated to break the most obstinate man, Burke manages to overpower his guard and withdrawing a miniaturized napalm rocket he has had secreted in a phoney boot-heel, he attacks the glass shield behind which The Leader cowers. The glass melts and Burke uses The Leader as a shield to rescue Elke and the Sherpa. They find the anthrax formula on microfilm, but before they can grab it, they are attacked again, and flee.

But as they break out of the plant, The Leader manages to throw Burke off, and escapes back inside. Burke grabs a sten machine-pistol from a guard and overcomes heavy opposition to get Elke and the Sherpa out. Once free, they make for the explosives Burke has cached, and Amos loads up, starts back for the plant. As he tops a rise, he is suddenly confronted by a quartet of the deadly Mongolian guards, each thrown-down on him with a machine-gun. They are about to spread him across the landscape, when almost magically, from behind them, rising up out of the snow-ridge behind which they have been concealed, four beautiful, but strong, Sherpa daughters erupt, and dispose of the guards with lightning-like judo chops.

Burke broken-field runs back to the plant, climbs up the face of the building, and plants his explosive in the blower system. He stretches out his fuse and lights it, but as he starts back, he sees a guard all bedecked with grenades and armor, pinching out the fuse. He rushes back as the Asian grabs the *plastique* from its berth. Burke fights with him, and in final desperation, pulls the pin on several grenades hanging on the guard's rig, and lifting guard, grenades, *plastique*, and all, he hurls the man into the great blower system. Then he makes a running dive away from the blower, hurls himself off the roof in a flat-out swan, and sinks halfway to his waist in a snowbank as the plant erupts in a pillar of fiery fury...

Later, after they have said goodbye to the Sherpa and his brood, Elke and Burke are trekking back to civilization when Elke voices her sadness that the only legacy her father left her, the formula, has been lost.

Abruptly, Burke laughs. He tells her he knows she managed to steal the microfilm from the bacteriophage lab while he was fighting off the Mongolians.

She draws a weapon, and laughs at him...*she* is Le Sauvage, top Russian spy-assassin, who has impersonated the long-since disposed-of Elke Losch, who has been using America's top secret agent to take all the risks, with her reaping the final benefits. She prepares to gun Burke down.

He calmly walks up to her as she clicks the trigger again and again on empty chambers. He lets her know he has been aware of her duplicity all along, had emptied the gun long before.

She cannot believe it, but Burke tells her the dossiers his agency gave him had indicated Elke Losch had been born blind, which was why Konrad Losch had been so amazed when Burke had told him she was watching out for the enemy in Budapest.

He takes her in tow, though she vows to escape and kill him, pledging herself as an implacable enemy no matter where he goes, nor how much he tries to escape her. We feel there is some substance to what she says, a woman as deadly as this, even as Amos Burke trudges off into the Tibetan mist with his lovely prisoner, Le Sauvage.

FADE OUT.

In the 31 January 1969 installment of *The Glass Teat*, Ellison recalled being interviewed by executive producer David Victor a year earlier about scripting a segment of *The Name of the Game*, the most expensive show on television. The wheel series featured a revolving cast of magazine men working for Howard Publications. Each week, the lead role in a 90-minute episode would be taken by Glenn Howard (Gene Barry of *Burke's Law* and its ill-fated spinoff, *Amos Burke, Secret Agent*), the publisher; Jeff Dillon (Tony Franciosa, later to star in *Curse of the Black Widow*—see BRAIN MOVIES, Volume 8—and Ellison's "Crazy as a Soup Sandwich" episode of *The Twilight Zone*), reporter for *People* magazine—six years before the real *People* hit the newsstands; or Dan Farrell (Robert Stack of *The Untouchables*), editor of *Crime* magazine.

Ellison completed a brief treatment titled "The Whimper of Whipped Dogs," before a big-screen commitment—*Best By Far* for Kubrick-producer James B. Harris—kept him from further developing the storyline for Stack's character. The treatment is the *earliest* use of an iconic Ellison title that would go on to be filmed as a 1971 episode of *The Young Lawyers* [as published in THE OTHER GLASS TEAT] before being reassigned to the *very different* Edgar Allan Poe Award-winning short story of 1974.

Note that Ellison refers to Dan Farrell by the actor's name, STACK, either for expediency or because the role had not yet been named at that early stage of pre-production.

As described in the aforementioned column, Ellison returned to *The Name of the Game* in January 1969, developing a treatment titled "Corridor Without Mirrors," concerning collegiate dissent, but a sampling of *au courant* broadcasts made the scenarist reconsider his subject matter. "They have killed the subject for any sensible and original attack. So I tore up the twenty-five pages of unfinished treatment in half, tore it in fourths, threw it in the circular file..." The preceding is no exaggeration; there is *no* evidence of "Corridor Without Mirrors" in Ellison's files, save for references to it in the column just quoted. "Smut"—the followup to "Corridor"—was completed, but never produced. [That treatment will appear in a forthcoming reissue of THE GLASS TEAT.]

The Whimper
of Whipped Dogs
The Name of the Game (1968)

Crime in the streets is not an isolated element of the contemporary scene. It is a patchwork quilt composed of many elements, and all of them connect back to the tenor of the times, to the attitudes of the people to the world in which they live: a world going steadily madder each day. Thirty-six good citizens watch in fascinated wonder as a madman stabs a woman to death in a gutter. Police, servants of the people, seemingly brutally attack peaceful demonstrators. Police doing their duty are beaten unconscious by revelers at marijuana parties. A man hangs poised on a ledge thirteen storeys above the concrete and a lunatic choir chants in unison. "Jump! Jump! Jump!" Black men hate white men...white men hate black men...and the gray man is caught in-between, riddled from both sides.

Are we indeed living in a time of madness?

Is the voice of the people becoming the whimper of whipped dogs?

What would we discover if we were to examine one city block in a steaming, tense, crime-filled period of summer heat and social unrest? Would we be able to isolate the bacillus of civil disobedience, the germ of hate, the sickness of fear and madness that threatens to tear every American city apart?

Truth is the name of the game.

Stack's assistant, the young writer, has gotten word from a Negro friend that the next week will see some "heavy action" in a melting-pot neighborhood of a large city. He has gone to Stack to tell him of this. Stack sees in this tip an opportunity to examine a cross-section of Americana under stress. By being on the scene, by involving himself and his assistant in the events about to transpire in that city block, he feels he will be able to provide *Now Magazine* with an unparalleled study of crime in the streets, civil unrest, the reasons for distrust of law enforcement agencies, racial tensions, all of the many volcanic encounters that have ripped the country for the past seven years.

His assistant expresses mild dislike for cops and the tactics they currently employ: dogs, cattle prods, mass retaliation, wanton brutality. Gene Barry, when the planned coverage is put to him, violently disagrees with the young man, takes the polarized opposite position: police are the only bulwark against anarchy, they are no less civil servants than postmen, yet no one shoots at a man carrying the mail. He feels the structure of morality and the values that forged this nation are in danger if the unlawful elements of society are allowed to run rampant under the hypocritical guise of freedom of speech or dissent. Their fiery exchange underscores the generation gap being forced to re-evaluate everything in which they've ever believed.

Already the story poses questions and answers.

Stack steps in between them. He suggests that police are merely the physical manifestation of the tenor of the culture. If we have a paranoid, psychopathic culture, then our law enforcers will reflect it. If ours is a society more and more coming to rely on violence, then they must reflect that, too. But he cannot believe that men sworn to protect the people can be thus morally corrupted. He senses that there is something dark and sinister walking the streets of today, and he proposes to examine it in this microcosmic universe of one city block.

In a way, he is challenging both Barry and his assistant to let him test their beliefs, where it counts, in a practical laboratory.

Barry agrees Stack has a hold on something potentially very exciting, terribly revealing, and perhaps conclusive.

Stack and his assistant go into that city block, and in much the same way as an Ed McBain police procedure novel, or a J. J. Marric suspense thriller, we see them involve themselves in a demonstration riot, a senseless street attack by teenage hoodlums on an old woman, a black power-oriented sniper attack, and the beating of a police officer making a routine arrest for marijuana possession.

These events do not happen sequentially, but seem to erupt all at once. Yet one triggers another, and in the growing lunacy in the streets Stack and his assistant begin to understand what it is that turns men into animals and a typical city street into a dark landscape of twisted mentalities and broken laws.

Within the dramatic framework of the danger and suspense of trying to keep the lid on the volcano threatening to erupt, we utilize Stack as the Rational Man, his assistants as the voice of the young dissidents, and from this semi-documentary approach we may begin to understand the nature of the crumbling life in which we live.

It is possible this show can be more than 90 minutes of entertainment that is forgotten as soon as the final credits are rolled.

It may serve as a warning and a service.

Even as it grips and mesmerizes an audience.

Peel the layers of madness from the gnarled black shadow that is our lunatic times, and we may find in the heart of it a hope of survival before we all go to our graves with the teeth of mad dogs in our throats.

The operable word for this kind of show might be: *Ambitious.*

After spending the bulk of 1970 on big-screen projects, Ellison was again lured back to the glass teat and found himself script editing *The Sixth Sense* for producer Stan Shpetner. As he recounted in the June 1985 installment of *Harlan Ellison's Watching*:

For seven weeks…I sold my soul to Universal Studios, then-president Lew Wasserman, a producer named Stan Shpetner, a primetime tv series called *The Sixth Sense*, the American Broadcasting Company, and anybody else who would make a reasonable bid on damaged goods…in short, I departed in a moment of greed and weakness from eleven years as a film and television *writer* to join the enemy on the other side of the desk. Yes, brethren and sistren, I became a story editor. Uck yichh choke!

As the Christ child's natal day celebration neared in that watershed year of 1971, I found myself standing in the stairwell between the eighth and ninth floors of the Black Tower, rattling the walls with Primal Screams that brought secretaries running from all directions to help the poor soul who was obviously being disemboweled. Soon thereafter, mere minutes later, I leaped onto Stan Shpetner's desk, did a deranged adagio, terminated my employment, and fled [series] television for a decade.

The series—based on the 1971 movie-of-the-week *Sweet, Sweet Rachel*—centered on parapsychologist Michael Rhodes (Gary Collins) and his assistant Nancy Murphy (Catherine Ferrar) as they investigated a different paranormal mystery each week. It ran for two seasons on ABC.

"Salamander"—presented herein—was Ellison's first contribution to *The Sixth Sense*. "Jeffrey's Being Quiet" [which appears in BRAIN MOVIES, Volume 4] his last.

Salamander

The Sixth Sense (19 November 1971)

In mythology they're known as "salamanders." Biological research has shown that under laboratory controlled conditions certain kinds of directed energy can be used to literally ignite the fatty tissue of the human body, causing virtual spontaneous combustion of human beings. See the Stanford research papers. In 1962, the US Army Chemical-Bacteriological Warfare experimental labs at Fort Ord conducted tests on children and adults (some of whom had thought they were involved with poltergeists) who were known to have caused fires to erupt without physical means. We are talking here about the documented, many-times-authenticated ESPower *known as* PYROTICISM. *The pyrotic—if we must have a scientific explanation—let's use the one the Army came up with—has the ability to control energy; energy he uses to increase the molecular vibration of atoms, thereby causing heat, producing fire. Pure mind power. Pure fire.*

Here is the story...

JASON KEARNEY wasn't that enthused about going to war. But he did it. To his horror, he found himself as the squirt man of a flamethrower team in the Nam. It did things to him. Roasting men alive in underground bunkers, the sound of their screams, the flames leaping up...

He couldn't take it. Battle fatigue the medics called it, but what it was all about was that Jason Kearney simply wasn't a violent man, and he couldn't hack it. So they mustered him out. Back into the real world, the quiet world, the peaceful world, to the one thing he had clung to during all those terrible months, his one link with sanity and grace, the one thing he loved the most—his wife, RACHEL.

They didn't bother telling him that while he was lying in a hospital bed in Tokyo, regaining his equilibrium, waiting to be released, his wife Rachel—like Catherine Genovese and so many others before her—had been knifed to death in a senseless act of street violence, in the courtyard of their high-rise apartment building, in full view of three dozen people...who had not cried out, who had not called the police, who had not lifted a hand to intervene, to stop the irrational, pointless street assault: they had merely watched.

But when Jason came back, and found out, it was too late to save his Rachel. Too late to do anything but hate the residents of the building... all of them...every last selfish, frightened, *uninvolved*, cold damned one of them who had let his wife, his sanity, his hope, bleed to death while they hid behind their curtained windows.

Jason has a relapse. They put him back in a hospital. Where he lies, seemingly catatonic. Never speaking, eyes open but unseeing, fed intravenously, but still *in* there somewhere, still hating.

What is ESP? Where does it come from? Do we all possess such powers, lying dormant in that unused seven-eighths of the brain we know nothing about, that *terra incognita* of the mind? Is it possible that under the most extreme pressures of mental torment those locked doors might open, and the power flow free?

If it's possible—and endless records say it is—surely one part of the answer lies in the mystery of will power. Men who have had their guts blown open, who should, by all rights, have died in some lonely place, have clung to life for days, weeks. *They had the power to live.* The will.

Jason Kearney has the will. Not merely to live...because what is life when everything one loves is gone...but the will for revenge. So potent, so indomitable, that the channels are opened, the power flows freely, and what has lain dormant, awakes. His thoughts are of the flamethrower team. The logical route for the power to take is through those memories, that obsession.

Jason Kearney becomes a pyrotic.

A salamander.

One night, soon after Jason's discovery of what had happened to his wife, a group of wealthy residents of the building are having an intimate little dinner party. They sit around the table talking about the terrible thing that happened in the courtyard, and the master of the household, a florid man with rationales, explains why he did nothing. Suddenly, as they lift their wine glasses, a high, piercing, eerie whine is heard, and the wine in the glasses bursts into flames. The punchbowl becomes a pillar of fire. The tablecloth catches. The entire apartment is a blistering inferno.

The next night a man slumped before a television set smells something strange, and his chair bursts into flames.

One after another, throughout the building, fires are wreaking havoc.

In one of the conflagrations, KATHERINE BATES saves a small child from a burning apartment, both her hands are seriously burned. Katherine Bates is romantically involved with DR. LUTHER RHODES.

The police and fire inspectors can find no answers. It is clearly not the work of an arsonist. Or if it is, he is a madman with a *modus operandi* that defies detection. Katherine comes to Rhodes. She has had enough contact with the labs, with Rhodes, with all the mysteries of ESP, to have heard of pyrotics. All other answers come up useless; perhaps this is one that works.

Rhodes moves in to assay the situation.

The salamander knows.

There is an attempt on Rhodes. Trapped in an elevator that suddenly bursts into flames.

He now knows there is a pyrotic phenomenon in operation, a salamander at work.

But who?

Who, of all the suspects in this building, can be the one? And why? And how can Rhodes stop him before there are more tragedies?

And when he does, finally, discover who is at the burning core of the terror, what does he find? A demon? A maniac? A malevolent criminal?

He finds a tortured, paralyzed man, locked into his own mind with bitterness and misery. How does he reach him...how does he put an end to the terror?

That is our story.

While developing *The Starlost* and *The Dark Forces* in 1972 [see PHOENIX WITHOUT ASHES and BRAIN MOVIES, Volume 5, respectively], Ellison took time out from his own projects to pitch a storyline titled "The Star" to *The Super*, a half-hour comedy starring Richard S. Castellano as Joe Girelli, superintendent of a New York City apartment building. Ten episodes were screened in the Summer of 1972, but Ellison's was not among them.

By the Spring of 1973, development on *The Dark Forces* had stalled and Ellison had fled from *The Starlost*, which was spiralling from brilliance (as evidenced by the pilot teleplay's winning of the WGA Award the following year) to banality (as displayed on the DVD release from VCI Entertainment). With the ill-fated series's scientific advisor, Ben Bova, still in tow, Ellison had set about adapting their collaborative short story, "Brillo," for NBC. [See BRAIN MOVIES, Volume 4.]

As the two men worked on the adaptation at Ellison's home, David Gerrold, then script editing the first season of *Land of the Lost*, visited and idly mentioned what a coup it would be if Ellison wrote a script for the series. Ellison disappeared into his office, leaving Gerrold to chat with Bova. Ellison reappeared a short time later with a treatment titled "The Guardians of the Pit," and presented it to Gerrold, knowing the story editor could never sell the outline to the network for reasons that will become apparent when you reach the end.

Gerrold's conversation with Bova was more fruitful as the latter *did* contribute a script titled "The Search" to *Land of the Lost*.

THE ELLISON TREATMENT concludes with a bit of *lagniappe*: a comic book plot for *Duck Tales* devised by Harlan *and Susan* Ellison at the request of Len Wein; the premise was filed amongst the television treatments, leading to considerable confusion for the editor, until a fax cover sheet with further information on the piece was located while finalizing this volume.

JASON DAVIS
Burbank, California
21 December 2018

The Star

The Super (13 April 1972)

Frankie is pursuing a lovely blonde with whom he went to school (a girl who is now working as a producer for educational tv). She mentions she wants to do a *very* low budget documentary on "life in the inner city, the cruel and crushing life of the average workingman." Frankie, trying to make points (and incidentally trying to get the twenty-five bucks as "research assistant" on the documentary) tells the girl he has just the thing: a rundown tenement building, with his brother Joe as super. The girl goes for it and Frankie hypes Joe and the family into being the subject of the show. At first Joe can't understand what's going on...him, Joe, on tv?...naw, that ain't right...on tv is Lorne Greene, is Mike Connors...tv isn't Joe Girelli. But by the end of act one, Frankie has him hyped and Joe begins to see himself as a star. Unfortunately, he doesn't *quite* know this is a documentary about slum life. So he cleans up the building. Works his ass off. Harasses the tenants to get things utterly ship-shape. And when the camera crew comes to shoot, it's spotless. So they can't do the show. Joe tries to drag in a street drunk to lie in the hall, tries to rent a rat, anything! But the Ms. who is producing tells him she can't use this place, it isn't dirty enough, and why did he try to fool them with a standard of living clearly above their norm. At which Joe gets the message: he's suddenly hip that he was supposed to be a symbol of degradation. And in the final lines he puts down the girl by saying this neighborhood, this building, this apartment may not be much, but it's their home, it's where he works and where he lives, and he's proud of it, and if she don't like it, she can go take her camera and shove it.

Fran—who has been dead against this all along—and the tenants look at Joe with new respect. He's more than their super: he's the spokesman (and in a way the guardian) of their little island in the city.

The Guardians of the Pit

Land of the Lost (1974)

ACT ONE:

Returning to a cave by the river they saw in an earlier segment, MARSHALL, WILL, and HOLLY enter, hoping it will offer an avenue of escape from The Land of the Lost. Once inside, however, they find the cave is shallow, and was once used as a storage place for wood and vines used by natives making rafts to glide down the river. They are about to leave, when one of the primordial beasts (to be designated) attacks them.

They rush back into the cave, and find they are trapped. Their situation seems hopeless until Holly perceives a draft of chill air blowing up from below, through a rift in the rocks. Using long chunks of ironwood, they begin hacking away at the hole until its true nature is revealed: the cave is merely the upper antechamber of a gigantic cavern below. A cavern so immense its dimensions cannot be discerned. A torch flung through the hole spirals down and down and is finally lost in utter darkness. And from below they can hear the strange and ominous sounds of...something...moving.

END ACT ONE

ACT TWO:

Realizing they cannot leave the cave, they resolve to build a pulley-&-platform from the ironwood, and from the vast store of strong vines in the chamber. They work for hours, all the while fending off the beast outside with their torches. Finally, they fall asleep, leaving Will to take the first spell at guarding the cave entrance. While they sleep, LIZARD MEN suddenly emerge from the hole in the cave's floor, and overpower Will. They drag him off, even as Marshall and Holly awake to his screams for help.

They have to go down to rescue him, but Holly cannot. She is agoraphobic, afraid of heights, and a descent on the platform terrifies her. But Marshall is stern with her, telling her now is the moment she must overcome her fear. *He* must stay to fight off the beast, and additionally the hole in the floor is not large enough for him to get through, though it is large enough for her...and time is of the essence. Both realize the Lizard Men are killers who may use Will for unspeakable practices. Holly agrees Marshall is right, but she is frightened. Yet this is the time when she must face her responsibilities as an emerging young adult.

They rig the platform and pulley, and Marshall lowers her. She begins the dizzying, long descent. Into the darkness. Down and down, swinging out over the bottomless chasm.

As she descends, the sounds heard from above take material form. The sounds made by the guardians of the pit...two giant pterodactyls, that swirl out of the darkness to attack her as she clings desperately to the platform, fighting for her life.

END ACT TWO

ACT THREE:

I tie everything up neatly. Trust me.

END ACT THREE

The Fowlness at the Center of the Earth!

by Harlan Ellison® & Susan Ellison
Duck Tales (12 August 1990)

Out of a dangerous and eerie casual encounter, Scrooge learns of the existence of the seven perfect giant rubies that adorn the collar of the three-headed dog Cerberus, who guards the portals to the Underworld.

From the encounter, Scrooge has come away with a mystic Talking Cube that tells him how to locate the portals. But it involves digging something like a TransAtlantic Tunnel. With the assistance of RoboDuck, a development of his Construction Company, Scrooge reaches the portals after many dangerous incidents made all the more terrifying because *something* is trying to stop them.

(What they do not know is that the "something" is actually the wonderful Carl Barks creation, The Phantom Blot, a strange inky mysterious villain.)

Once at the portals, they are stopped by forces of ancient angry Greek gods, who say the only way they can get that collar is if they complete the fabled 7 Labors of Quackules.

RoboDuck both helps and hinders their progress, as Scrooge, the nephews, Launchpad (and any other characters we think will be useful to us) descend into the center of the Earth, the fabled Underworld of mythology, to help the inept yet powerful Quackules complete his

Labors, thus freeing him from the eternity-long prison to which he's been consigned.

HARLAN ELLSON has been characterized by *The New York Times Book Review* as having "the spellbinding quality of a great nonstop talker, with a cultural warehouse for a mind."

The Los Angeles Times suggested, "It's long past time for Harlan Ellison to be awarded the title: 20th century Lewis Carroll." And the *Washington Post Book World* said simply, "One of the great living American short story writers."

He has written or edited 118 books; more than 1700 stories, essays, articles, and newspaper columns; two dozen teleplays, for which he received the Writers Guild of America most outstanding teleplay award for solo work an unprecedented four times; and a dozen movies. *Publishers Weekly* called him "Highly Intellectual." (Ellison's response: "Who, Me?"). He won the Mystery Writers of America Edgar Allan Poe award twice, the Horror Writers Association Bram Stoker award six times (including The Lifetime Achievement Award in 1996), the Nebula award of the Science Fiction Writers of America five times (including the Grand Master Award), the Hugo Award 8 ½ times, and received the Silver Pen for Journalism from P.E.N. Not to mention the World Fantasy Award; the British Fantasy Award; the American Mystery Award; plus two Audie Awards and two Grammy nominations for Spoken Word recordings.

He created great fantasies for the 1985 CBS revival of *The Twilight Zone* (including Danny Kaye's final performance) and *The Outer Limits*; traveled with The Rolling Stones; marched with Martin Luther King from Selma to Montgomery; created roles for Buster Keaton, Wally Cox, Gloria Swanson, and nearly 100 other stars on *Burke's Law*; ran with a kid gang in Brooklyn's Red Hook to get background for his first novel; covered race riots in Chicago's "back of the yards" with the late James Baldwin; sang with, and dined with, Maurice Chevalier; once stood off the son of the Detroit Mafia kingpin with a Remington XP-100 pistol-rifle, while wearing nothing but a bath towel; sued Paramount and ABC-TV for plagiarism and won $337,000. His most recent legal victory, in protection of copyright against global Internet piracy of writers' work, in May of 2004—a four-year-long litigation against AOL et al.—has resulted in revolutionizing protection of creative properties on the web. (As promised, he has repaid hundreds of contributions [totaling $50,000] from the KICK Internet Piracy support fund.) But the bottom line, as voiced by *Booklist*, is this: "One thing for sure: the man can write."

He lived with his wife, Susan, inside The Lost Aztec Temple of Mars, in Los Angeles.

CHRONOLOGY OF BOOKS BY
HARLAN ELLISON®
1958 – 2019

SHORT STORY COLLECTIONS:

THE DEADLY STREETS [1958]

SEX GANG (as "Paul Merchant") [1959]

A TOUCH OF INFINITY [1960]

CHILDREN OF THE STREETS [1961]

GENTLEMAN JUNKIE
and Other Stories of the Hung-Up Generation [1961]

ELLISON WONDERLAND [1962/2015]

PAINGOD and Other Delusions [1965]

I HAVE NO MOUTH & I MUST SCREAM [1967]

FROM THE LAND OF FEAR [1967]

LOVE AIN'T NOTHING BUT SEX MISSPELLED [1968]

THE BEAST THAT SHOUTED LOVE
AT THE HEART OF THE WORLD [1969]

OVER THE EDGE [1970]

ALL THE SOUNDS OF FEAR (British publication only) [1973]

DE HELDEN VAN DE HIGHWAY (Dutch publication only) [1973]

APPROACHING OBLIVION [1974]

THE TIME OF THE EYE (British publication only) [1974]

DEATHBIRD STORIES [1975/2011]

NO DOORS, NO WINDOWS [1975]

HOE KAN IK SCHREEUWEN ZONDER MOND
(Dutch publication only) [1977]

STRANGE WINE [1978]

SHATTERDAY [1980]

STALKING THE NIGHTMARE [1982]

ANGRY CANDY [1988]

ENSAMVÄRK (Swedish publication only) [1992]

JOKES WITHOUT PUNCHLINES [1995]

BCE ЗВУКИ СТРАХА (ALL FEARFUL SOUNDS)
(Unauthorized Russian publication only) [1997]

THE WORLDS OF HARLAN ELLISON
(Authorized Russian publication only) [1997]

SLIPPAGE: Precariously Poised, Previously Uncollected Stories [1997]

KOLETIS, KES KUULUTAS ARMASTUST MAAILMA SLIDAMES
(Estonian publication only) [1999]

LA MACHINE AUX YEUX BLEUS (French publication only) [2001]

TROUBLEMAKERS [2001]

PTAK ŚMIERCI (THE BEST OF HARLAN ELLISON)
(Polish publication only) [2003]

PULLING A TRAIN [2012]

GETTING IN THE WIND [2012]

PEBBLES FROM THE MOUNTAIN [2015]

CAN AND CAN'TANKEROUS (edited by Jason Davis) [2015]

COFFIN NAILS [2016]

NOVELS:

WEB OF THE CITY [1958]

THE SOUND OF A SCYTHE [1960]

SPIDER KISS [1961]

BLOOD'S A ROVER
(edited by Jason Davis) [2018]

SHORT NOVELS:

DOOMSMAN [1967]

ALL THE LIES THAT ARE
MY LIFE [1980]

RUN FOR THE STARS [1991]

MEFISTO IN ONYX [1993]

OMNIBUS VOLUMES:

THE FANTASIES OF
HARLAN ELLISON [1979]

DREAMS WITH SHARP TEETH [1991]

THE GLASS TEAT &
THE OTHER GLASS TEAT [2011]

COLLABORATIONS:

PARTNERS IN WONDER:
Collaborations with 14 Other Wild Talents [1971]

THE STARLOST: Phoenix Without Ashes
(with Edward Bryant) [1975]

MIND FIELDS: 33 Stories Inspired by the Art of Jacek Yerka [1994]

I HAVE NO MOUTH, AND I MUST SCREAM:
The Interactive CD-Rom
(Co-Designed with David Mullich and David Sears) [1995]

"REPENT, HARLEQUIN!" SAID THE TICKTOCKMAN
(rendered with paintings by Rick Berry) [1997]

2000X (Host and Creative Consultant
of National Public Radio episodic series) [2000–2001]

HARLAN ELLISON'S MORTAL DREADS
(dramatized by Robert Armin) [2012]

SCREENPLAYS & SUCHLIKE:

THE ILLUSTRATED HARLAN ELLISON
(edited by Byron Preiss) [1978]

HARLAN ELLISON'S MOVIE [1990]

I, ROBOT: The Illustrated Screenplay
(based on Isaac Asimov's story-cycle) [1994]

THE CITY ON THE EDGE OF FOREVER [1996]

RETROSPECTIVES:

ALONE AGAINST TOMORROW: A 10-Year Survey [1971]

THE ESSENTIAL ELLISON: A 35-Year Retrospective
(edited by Terry Dowling,
with Richard Delap & Gil Lamont) [1987]

THE ESSENTIAL ELLISON: A 50-Year Retrospective
(edited by Terry Dowling) [2001]

UNREPENTANT: A Celebration of the Writing of
Harlan Ellison (edited by Robert T. Garcia) [2010]

THE TOP OF THE VOLCANO:
The Award-Winning Stories of Harlan Ellison [2014]

THE HARLAN ELLISON DISCOVERY SERIES:

STORMTRACK by James Sutherland [1975]

AUTUMN ANGELS by Arthur Byron Cover [1975]

THE LIGHT AT THE END OF THE UNIVERSE
by Terry Carr [1976]

ISLANDS by Marta Randall [1976]

INVOLUTION OCEAN by Bruce Sterling [1978]

MOTION PICTURE (DOCUMENTARY):

DREAMS WITH SHARP TEETH
(A Film About Harlan Ellison
produced and directed by Erik Nelson) [2009]

CHRONOLOGY OF BOOKS BY
HARLAN ELLISON®
1958 – 2019

GRAPHIC NOVELS:

DEMON WITH A GLASS HAND
(adaptation with Marshall Rogers) [1986]

NIGHT AND THE ENEMY
(adaptation with Ken Steacy) [1987]

VIC AND BLOOD: *The Chronicles/Continuing
Adventures of a Boy and His Dog*
(adaptation by Richard Corben) [1989/2003]

HARLAN ELLISON'S DREAM CORRIDOR,
Volumes One & Two [1996/2007]

PHOENIX WITHOUT ASHES [2010/2011]
(art by Alan Robinson and John K. Snyder III)

HARLAN ELLISON'S 7 AGAINST CHAOS
(art by Paul Chadwick and Ken Steacy) [2013]

THE CITY ON THE EDGE OF FOREVER:
The Original Teleplay (adaptation by Scott Tipton &
David Tipton, art by J.K. Woodward) [2014/2015]

BATMAN '66: *The Lost Episode* (adaptation by Len Wein,
art by Joe Prado and José García-López) [2014]

AUDIOBOOKS:

THE VOICE FROM THE EDGE: I HAVE NO MOUTH,
AND I MUST SCREAM (Vol. One) [1999]

THE VOICE FROM THE EDGE: MIDNIGHT
IN THE SUNKEN CATHEDRAL (Vol. Two) [2001]

RUN FOR THE STARS [2005]

THE VOICE FROM THE EDGE: PRETTY
MAGGIE MONEYEYES (Vol. Three) [2009]

THE VOICE FROM THE EDGE: THE DEATHBIRD
& OTHER STORIES (Vol. Four) [2011]

THE VOICE FROM THE EDGE: SHATTERDAY
& OTHER STORIES (Vol. Five) [2011]

ELLISON WONDERLAND [2015]

WEB AND THE CITY [2015]

SPIDER KISS [2015]

THE CITY ON THE EDGE OF FOREVER
(full-cast dramatization) [2016]

ON THE ROAD WITH HARLAN ELLISON:

ON THE ROAD WITH HARLAN ELLISON
(Vol. One) [1983/2001]

ON THE ROAD WITH HARLAN ELLISON (Vol. Two) [2004]

ON THE ROAD WITH HARLAN ELLISON (Vol. Three) [2007]

ON THE ROAD WITH HARLAN ELLISON (Vol. Four) [2011]

ON THE ROAD WITH HARLAN ELLISON:
His Last Big Con (Vol. Five) [2011]

ON THE ROAD WITH HARLAN ELLISON:
The Grand Master Edition (Vol. Six) [2012]

ON THE ROAD WITH HARLAN ELLISON (Vol. Seven) [2018]

THE WHITE WOLF SERIES:

EDGEWORKS 1: OVER THE EDGE & AN EDGE IN MY VOICE [1996]

EDGEWORKS 2: SPIDER KISS
& STALKING THE NIGHTMARE [1996]

EDGEWORKS 3: THE HARLAN ELLISON HORNBOOK
& HARLAN ELLISON'S MOVIE [1997]

EDGEWORKS 4: LOVE AIN'T NOTHING BUT SEX MISSPELLED &
THE BEAST THAT SHOUTED LOVE AT
THE HEART OF THE WORLD [1997]

AS EDITOR:

DANGEROUS VISIONS [1967/2002]

NIGHTSHADE & DAMNATIONS:
The Finest Stories of Gerald Kersh [1968]

AGAIN, DANGEROUS VISIONS [1972]

MEDEA: *Harlan's World* [1985]

JACQUES FUTRELLE'S
"THE THINKING MACHINE"
STORIES [2003]

NON-FICTION & ESSAYS:

MEMOS FROM PURGATORY [1961]

THE GLASS TEAT: *Essays of Opinion on Television* [1970]

THE OTHER GLASS TEAT: *Further Essays of
Opinion on Television* [1975]

THE BOOK OF ELLISON (edited by Andrew Porter) [1978]

SLEEPLESS NIGHTS IN THE PROCRUSTEAN BED
(edited by Marty Clark) [1984]

AN EDGE IN MY VOICE [1985]

HARLAN ELLISON'S WATCHING [1989]

THE HARLAN ELLISON HORNBOOK [1990]

BUGF#CK! *The Useless Wit & Wisdom of Harlan Ellison*
(edited by Arnie Fenner) [2011]

HARLAN ELLISON BOOKS PRESERVATION PROJECT

THE DIMENSIONS OF HARLAN ELLISON [2019]

THE EPHEMERAL ELLISON [2019]

THE ELLISON TREATMENT [2019]

THIS BOOK NEEDS NO INTRODUCTION
BY HARLAN ELLISON [2019]

**EDGEWORKS ABBEY OFFERINGS
(Edited by Jason Davis):**

BRAIN MOVIES: *The Original Teleplays of
Harlan Ellison* (Vol. One) [2011]

BRAIN MOVIES: *The Original Teleplays of
Harlan Ellison* (Vol. Two) [2011]

HARLAN 101: *Encountering Ellison* [2011]

THE SOUND OF A SCYTHE *and 3
Brilliant Novellas* [2011]

ROUGH BEASTS: *Seventeen Stories Written
Before I Got Up To Speed* [2012]

NONE OF THE ABOVE [2012]

BRAIN MOVIES: *The Original Teleplays of
Harlan Ellison* (Vol. Three) [2013]

BRAIN MOVIES: *The Original Teleplays of
Harlan Ellison* (Vol. Four) [2013]

BRAIN MOVIES: *The Original Teleplays of
Harlan Ellison* (Vol. Five) [2013]

HONORABLE WHOREDOM
AT A PENNY A WORD [2013]

AGAIN, HONORABLE WHOREDOM
AT A PENNY A WORD [2014]

BRAIN MOVIES: *The Original Teleplays of
Harlan Ellison* (Vol. Six) [2014]

HARLAN ELLISON'S ENDLESSLY WATCHING [2014]

8 IN 80 BY ELLISON (guest edited by Susan Ellison) [2014]

THE LAST PERSON TO MARRY A DUCK
LIVED 300 YEARS AGO [2016]

BRAIN MOVIES: *The Original Teleplays of
Harlan Ellison* (Vol. Seven) [2016]

BRAIN MOVIES: *The Original Teleplays of
Harlan Ellison* (Vol. Eight) [2019]

BRAIN MOVIES *Presents* BLOOD'S A ROVER [2019]

FOE: *Friends of Ellison* [2019]

WHY DO YOU CALL ME ISHMAEL WHEN
YOU KNOW MY NAME IS BERNIE? [2019]

The Harlan Ellison® Books Preservation Project
was made possible by

Gary Wallen
Andrew Hackard
Jay Kemp
John Farmer
Stanley L. Korwin
Sven-Hendrik Magotsch
Dan Melin
Jay Corsetti
Eliot R. Weinstein
James Bocchinfuso
David Loftus
Stanford Maxwell Brown
William M Feero
William Dennehy
Mark L Cohen
Curt M Snyder
Rod Searcey
John Palagyi
Suzzii Barrafato, P. Stashio Nutz & Tortoni Spumoni & Co.
Dan McCormick
Andy Bustamante
Samantha A. Vitagliano
Mike Jacka
Alice Tatarian
David Jessup & family
Paul Guay & Susan S. Knight
J. Michael Straczynski
Raymond McCauley
David M. Barsky
Gordon H. Schnaper
Joel T. & Carole Hampton Cotter
Gerald R. Parham
Michael J. Dymond, MD
and 725 other Friends of Ellison.